TEACHING WITHIN PRISON WALLS
A Thematic History

Thom Gehring, Ph.D. and Carolyn Eggleston, Ph.D.

Published by

**CALIFORNIA STATE UNIVERSITY
SAN BERNARDINO**

Published in San Bernardino, California,
by California State University, San Bernardino.

Special thanks for the support from the California Department of Corrections and Rehabilitation, Division of Juvenile Justice Education Unit.

New material copyright © 2007 by Thom. Gehring and Carolyn Eggleston.

How this Book is Presented

The California State University, San Bernrdino mountain logo indicates when an entry ends, so the next one can be expected. We hope this will move readers easily through the book's transitions.

Without limiting the rights under copyright reserved above, no part of this publication may be reproduced, stored in or introduced into a retrieval system, or transmitted, in any form or by any means (electronic, mechanical, photocopying, recording or otherwise), without the prior written permission of both the copyright owner and the above publisher of this book.

The scanning, uploading, and distribution of this book via the Internet or via any other means without the written permission of the publisher is illegal and punishable by law. Please purchase only authorized electronic editions and do not participate in or encourage electronic piracy of copyrightable materials. Your support of the authors' rights is appreciated.

Cover design and typesetting by Deanna Dunn

Photo on cover and page iv is reprinted with permission from the Osborne family papers, Special Collections Research Center, Syracuse University Library. (See p.iv for additional information.)

Printed in the United States of America by
Wirz & Company Printing
444 Colton Avenue
Colton, CA 92324

ISBN 0-9776008-2-3

This book is printed on permanent/durable paper.

Abstract

1. 1787-1875: Sabbath school period; Pennsylvania (solitary) and Auburn (factory) systems of prison management; correctional education is recognized as possible.

2. 1876-1900: Zebulon Brockway's tenure at Elmira Reformatory; based on the work of Maconochie (prison reform in the South Pacific), Crofton (Irish prison reform), and the Pilsburys (prison management in the U.S.); the beginnings of correctional/special education; reformatory movement efforts to transform prisons into schools.

3. 1901-1929: Libraries, reformatories for women, and democracy. Thomas Mott Osborne, Katherine Bement Davis, and Austin MacCormick.

4. 1930-1940: The golden age of correctional education; early influence of MacCormick, especially in the New York and Federal Bureau of Prisons experiments; rebirth of correctional/special education.

5. 1941-1945: World War II, which interrupted the development of correctional education.

6. 1946-1963: Limited recovery from the interruption.

7. 1964-1980: "Hot spots" in correctional education—the Federal influence in education; postsecondary programs; correctional school districts; special education legislation; correctional teacher preparation programs.

8. 1981-1988: Conservative trend in Federal programs and many states; rise of the Correctional Education Association's influence; continued refinement of trends from the previous period.

9. 1989- : The current period; Canadian Federal paradigm; contributions by the Ross and Fabiano team, Stephen Duguid, David Werner, and others; greater international cooperation.

This photo is of a painting of Thomas Mott Osborne, as he appeared in 1913 during his voluntary incarceration at New York State's Auburn Prison—to learn the prison business. Many prisoners knew him as Inmate Tom Brown, #3164 (see p 46).

Osborne's book about his time at Auburn was entitled, *Within Prison Walls,* (1924a). Another book, by Wallack, Kendall, and Briggs, *Education Within Prison Walls,* (1939), announced progress that had been realized in New York State correctional education programs. The current volume is called, *Teaching Within Prison Walls,* to indicate to knowledgeable readers that its authors identify as part of that same school of thought (see p. 70).

CONTENTS

Abstract .... Page   iii

Foreward by Margaret Puffer. vi

Preface viii

1789-1875 1

1879-1900 31

1901-1929 42

1930-1941 63

1941-1945 74

1947-1963 76

1964-1980 78

1981-1988 87

1980-the Present 94

References 103

Acknowledgements 106

Foreword
by Margaret Puffer

My introduction to correctional education came through the field of special education. During my course work for a masters degree in what Minnesotans call emotionally disturbed and behavior disordered youth (E/BD; in other parts of the country it is often called severe emotional disturbance or SED), my student teaching placement was in SPAN, a pull-out junior high school program with IEPs. My advisor was Dr. Frank Wood, who had helped establish the *Journal of Emotional and Behavior Disorders in Youth*. He was also deeply involved in the struggle for passage of PL 94-142, the Education of All Handicapped Children Act. As I learned about the 94-142 Law, I also discovered where these students were housed—a level four program (on a school grounds with locked doors to prevent other students from entering). Level four students were locked in to protect them, but the result in some ways was similar to a traditional confinement situation. I would later move to California, where special education is non-categorical, and where my E/BD preparation would land me a job teaching students with severe and profound physical disabilities. I asked where I would work with students with emotional disabilities, and was told that I would have to work at a juvenile hall.

My story is like those of my peers in correctional education. I simply found myself there. But, unlike my peers, I was following what I was trained to do in my teacher preparation program.

I was misunderstood by the people around me—they seemed unfamiliar with cognitive and behavioral techniques, and with social learning theory—and they could not account for my success in classroom management. I was so confounded by this confinement context that I returned to Minnesota to seek assistance from Dr. Wood. He directed me to the *Journal of Correctional Education*, and I spent many summer evenings reading back editions cover to cover, in the old stacks at the University of Minnesota's Walker Library. Eventually the work of Stephen Duguid, Carolyn Eggleston, and Thom Gehring emerged as representing a philosophy to approach the context of my work with students in confinement. A twenty year relationship of reading, training, and dialogue in correctional education had begun.

I became a mentor teacher. My colleagues, who were encountering the same concerns that had started me on my quest, asked, "What have you got for me? Where can I learn more about the work I am doing daily 'inside.'" So one of the requests I made was to have my peers at juvenile hall, and other teachers outside, prepared in correctional education. Unknown to me, an administrator in the juvenile hall program had requested a meeting with others from nearby systems who were encountering the same concerns. In the elevator of a county schools office in an adjacent county, I met Carolyn Eggleston and Thom Gehring. We all felt as if we had already met—because we all represented the same school of thought.

That meeting marked the origin of the Alternative and Correctional Education Academy, which was founded on scholarly groundwork by Richard Ashcroft. Eventually three cohorts emerged from the Academy, two in Orange County and one in San Bernardino County, California. A third Academy is emerging in California's Division of Juvenile Justice, formerly the California Youth Authority. These academies are for institutional educators who want to meet recredentialling requirements by focusing on correctional education, as opposed to one of the related fields (special education, reading, vocational education, and so on).

One of the first courses I took at the Orange County Academy was a foundations course on the history and literature of correctional education. It was taught by Thom Gehring and Carolyn Eggleston. I enjoyed that course. In 2006 Gehring and Eggleston had a book published, *Correctional Education Chronology*, which presents important details about prison reform and correctional education to which every correctional educator should have access.

That book is complemented by the current volume, *Teaching Within Prison Walls: A Thematic History*. I found this volume provides good summaries of the details in the *Chronology*. It is conversational in tone, and is really very much like the lectures and discussions we had in that foundations course. My hope is that it will be as valuable for you as it has been for me.

Margaret Puffer, Senior Fellow
Center for the Study of Correctional Education
California State University
San Bernardino, CA 92407

Preface

This is a thematic history of correctional education and prison reform. It is one version of the narrative or lecture(s) that might accompany the course on this subject, Foundations of Institutional Education: History and Literature. The narrative focuses on North American correctional education during the 1787-1987 period, but also introduces some events from other times and places. Alternate versions of this narrative might include the same basic themes, but elaborations with different details might be made. Most of the details from this narrative are available in the *Correctional Education Chronology*, by Gehring and Eggleston (San Bernardino: CA State University, 2006). Like the field of correctional education, this narrative varies according to interpretation.

All the information in the narrative is connected, not only to itself, but also to the unfolding human drama. It is connected to the work of people such as Albert Einstein, Clara Barton, and Franklin Delano Roosevelt; to prison management, prison reform, and to reform in the most general sense; to local schools, universities, labor unions, factories, and libraries; to war, brutality, imperialism, genocide, racism, and sexism; to bureaucracy, courage, failure, and to other high stakes, life and death concerns.

It was a pleasure to prepare the narrative, like visiting old friends in the prison reform and correctional education school of thought. It was also a chance to reflect on our current interpretations and the things we learned since the last time we wrote about this topic. We do not pretend to understand it all, but we have gradually learned that working on this topic is good for us, somehow related to our dispositions toward the world. This is a grand adventure, because there are always "new" things to learn: books to read of which we were previously ignorant, new relationships between the things we did know, new emphases that accrue from current tasks.

Although we have been pursuing the history of correctional education for decades, there are many things about the history of prison reform and correctional education that we do not know. If readers become aware of an important theme that is not addressed herein, we hope they will let us know. We can be reached through the following:

Thom Gehring, Ph.D. and Carolyn Eggleston, Ph.D., Directors
Center for the Study of Correctional Education
California State University, San Bernardino, CA 92407
Thom's phone: (909) 537-5653; FAX: (909) 882-3015; e-mail: tgehring@csusb.edu
Carolyn's phone: (909) 537-5654; FAX: (909) 537-7011; e-mail: egglesto@csusb.edu

Dedication

This work is dedicated to the correctional education heroes who came before, and upon whose shoulders we stand. We thank you.   April, 2007.

The 1787-1875 Period

Introduction

People often inquire about the differences and similarities between correctional education and education in local community schools. This interest may be a helpful way to begin a narrative on the history of correctional education. Another book on educational administration (McMillan and Schumacher, 2001) indicates that three cultural aspirations shaped American local schools over the centuries: liberty, equality, and efficiency. The present authors found this synthesis informative and encouraging. It certainly suggests a great deal about the American spirit and an important social process that it shaped. However, the McMillan and Schumacher synthesis does not describe the forces that have "driven" correctional education for more than 200 years. The differences between correctional education and local public schools may accrue from cultural differences. America has a double standard. Reform warden Thomas Mott Osborne urged us to consider a single rather than a double standard. Perhaps one of the most relevant questions we should consider is, "Is the quality of this school like one in which you would want your child educated?"

Three pervasive influences have shaped correctional education throughout its history, and they are quite different from the influences Guthrie and Reed cited: overcrowding, institutionalization, and reform. They are the same influences that have shaped the configuration of the entire juvenile and adult corrections industry. These influences have sometimes been experienced sequentially and sometimes in combination.

Overcrowding pertains not merely to institutional overpopulation, but also to the largest urban/industrial centers, where the rising expectations of the poorest community members clash with those who are wealthier. Institutional-minded thinking can be a polite euphemism for authoritarianism, brutality, physical coercion, and bureaucratic manipulation. Reform is the element that balances life and makes it more tolerable—it is rooted in the aspiration to improve the human condition.

The entire scope and magnitude of institutions for confined juveniles and adults can be explained entirely by the domination of these three factors. Correctional education is a branch of prison reform, but it has been impacted by, (a) overcrowding and, (b) badgered by institutionalization throughout its distinct historical periods. It has also been continuously blessed by, (c) the spirit of reform. This chapter presents the story of how correctional education came into its current configuration, and how it may yet develop.

Historical Context

There were always prisons of some sort, mostly dungeons for political prisoners, like the Bastille or the Tower of London. Apart from these exceptions, ancient and medieval prisons were not used to confine or warehouse criminals as we use them today. Instead, they were places to hold people before they received corporal punishment, or were executed, or both.

Prisons in the modern sense only emerged during the 16th century, a result of several changing conditions. Leprosy subsided; the need for lazar houses or lazarios (hospitals for lepers) declined. Monastic life also declined, and monasteries were frequently left vacant. With abandoned institutional facilities suddenly available, Europeans converted many of them into prisons. As is the case today, they frequently provided an economic base for the community.

This pattern is central to the origins of correctional education. Prisons began in the spirit of reform. Correctional education and prison reform share the same goal: to reform prisoners and prisons. The transformation of prisons into schools is an historic theme of prison reform, but prison reform could not begin until there were prisons. In the grand sweep of Western history then, correctional education is a new wrinkle—despite the fact that it has been in place for more than 200 years.

Before prisons torture, mutilation (usually branding or the chopping off of hands or ears), debilitating fines, exile, public humiliation, and death were the socially preferred responses to crime. Eventually, society sickened at the sheer magnitude of officially sanctioned bloodletting and brutality. Modern prisons originated as a reform-oriented attempt to end the horrible, and often very visible physical suffering inflicted on people identified as criminals, and on their families. To this extent, prisons began as an expression of Western civilization's humanistic dream.

The Institutionalization of a Noble Idea

However, applications of the new idea did not live up to the high expectations of reformers. Torture typified this problem. Torture predated prisons, but was adopted "inside" once the prisons were established. Torture became institutionalized.

Modern readers may be unaware of the kinds of organized torture that were used routinely in prisons, and of its pervasive influence. Prison "keepers" designed all sorts of machines and implements of destruction and torment to maintain order and control. Chains, cages, treadmills, dark cells, heat treatments, deprivation of normal diet, and so forth, were creatively applied. Even the relatively tame modes of torture seem absurd to us now. Cold dunking was a continuous shower, to make breathing very labored and difficult. A parallel procedure for women was called the cold douche. But flogging was the main torture procedure. The literature is replete with details about various types of flogging, the associated implements, and its results on the human body and psyche.

There were various types of whips and straps, each designed to inflict a different type of wound. Generally a physician was assigned to monitor the convict's pulse and make sure he did not die prematurely. Flogging led to several problems. One was that the action of the whip removed the skin and frequently exposed the spine. Another was that a great deal of blood was lost. Various procedures were developed to keep up the torture without killing the person. Constant vigilance was required to implement a prescribed number of lashes without killing the convict. Sometimes the procedure had to be applied incrementally.

The early and continuing impact of torture on prison culture can be traced by its application at a particular prison The whipping post at Delaware's New Castle Prison was famous by 1868. It remained in place until 1954, though out of use since World War II. Nevertheless, the post was reinstalled in the mid-1980s, as a silent reminder to inmates.

It did not matter that prisons were designed specifically to avoid torture; they inherently facilitated brutality. This first period provides our first example of the institutionalization problem.

The term "institutionalization" is most frequently used to describe the individual behavior of incarcerates. However, institutionalization is evident in the behavior of staff and systems, as well. It consists of the application of old strategies, even in a new setting where they might not be needed—the over-reliance on past practice. The use of torture in prisons was an early indicator that prisons actually created more problems than they could solve.

John Howard, who worked just after the American Revolution, was the father of prison reform. He identified this issue with clarity. He was the first active, visible, respected expert who advocated that society rethink its prison dream. Evidence suggested the dream had become a nightmare. Institutionalization soured the high aims that originally led to the establishment of prisons. Howard's most revered contributions were made in England—a period of English penal history that would have far-reaching effects on prisons and prison reform all over the world. That period was driven by the overcrowding problem.

<u>Lasting Effects of Overcrowding</u>

The great displacements during the industrial revolution resulted in massive urbanization and fostered conditions that spawned crime. Consistent with its mercantile philosophy of economics the British Parliament steadfastly refused to expend funds on prisons and prison construction. Instead, Britain populated America with criminals. A huge proportion of American colonists were criminals. England had a New World frontier, and indentured servitude gradually became preferred over torture. It provided an "escape valve" for perceived dangerous persons. Indentured servitude got the criminals out of England, and relocated them in a place where they might actually become useful.

The customs regulating indentured servitude varied from colony to colony, and from time to time, but it was an important factor in all the English colonies of North America, where a severe labor shortage characterized the economy. Georgia was established in 1733, specifically as a penal colony. English crime soared when gin was legalized in 1735. Wave upon wave of Britain's poor and dangerous classes migrated to America, many under pressure of coercion.

The American Revolution posed an extremely serious dilemma for Britain, one that modern scholars frequently neglect. The Colonies could no longer serve as a repository for criminals and riffraff. What were the British to do with them all? In desperation, Parliament seized upon a quick fix solution, instead of coming to terms with the issue. It implemented the hulk system.

Hulks were exactly what their name implied—the old rotting hulks of wooden ships that had outlived their usefulness on the open sea. Masts were removed and decks were divided and subdivided into small cells with low ceilings. Hulks were floating prisons and jails, chained to harbor docks. They were cramped; men were unable to stand up in their cells.

The "trickle down" theory was applied in earnest here. Most hulks had no sanitary facilities, so human waste trickled down through the cracks of the old, rotting decks. Convicts assigned to the top decks had a reasonable chance of staying alive for a while. However, convicts assigned to the lower decks lived with raw sewage dripping down all the time. Their lives were cut short by disease; the prisoner "turnover rate" was high.

Just as this trend was unfolding, a man named John Howard was elected sheriff of Bedford, England. One of his new responsibilities was to manage the local gaol. In England the g-a-o-l spelling was used, as opposed to the American j-a-i-l. Howard did not know anything about gaols. Upon inspection, he abhorred the facility's condition.

Early gaols were chaotic. They predated the classification of prisoners. Young people and old people, males and females, first offenders and hardened criminals were all thrown together in the same, shared space. The gaol scene was frequently described as a state of "riotous debauchery." This was a terrible management problem, and it made prison reform very difficult.

Classification is the precondition for all institutional programming, including education. Without the classification of incarcerates according to gender, age, criminal experience, personal attributes, and so forth, all programming efforts would be absurd. Identified or targeted inmates could not be placed in appropriate programs. For example, what value is a program for sex offenders if sex offenders are not identified and matched with the program location? The same applies for education and all other programs. It is impossible to maintain a useful education program without an effective system of classification and movement.

John Howard's Reform Efforts

Howard began a series of visits around Great Britain and Europe, to learn the attributes of well managed gaols. Then he wrote several reports and recommendations about how to manage a successful gaol. There is some dispute regarding one of Howard's recommendations, but his reports were generally received as the state-of-the-art documents on prison reform. The man had credibility.

John Howard's most widely circulated report supported three major improvements. First, gaolers should be salaried. Gaolers lived on what they could charge inmates and their families, in the form of high fees for food, medical attention, liquor, and so forth. Often the gaolers employed female offenders in prostitution rings based in the institutions. Howard found these conditions unacceptable. Salaries for gaolers were seen as the first step toward a solution.

Second, Howard recommended that some classification scheme should be implemented. Riotous debauchery and the resultant injuries, damage, and pregnancies were simply deplorable. Howard did not have clarity about what programming might be applied (for example, he did not advocate correctional education—may not have even thought of it), but he knew that prisoners should be classified, at least by age and gender.

Third, Howard recommended that all prisoners should be confined separately, to prevent "contamination by crime." When prisoners lived together in the same space, they used their time to discuss crime strategies. Gaols became schools for vice, another unacceptable situation. Solitary confinement, with a rule against talking, was the obvious solution. It was this recommendation that produced the most controversy, since Howard advocated this differently throughout his life. However, he consistently cited specific "solitary gaols" around Europe as prototypic models, and he supported leaders who advocated solitary confinement.

John Howard's three recommendations were held in high regard. Howard's systematic visitations qualified his report as the best available guidance on how to manage a successful gaol. No one else could match his expertise. In addition to international research, Howard had been incarcerated himself by the French as a prisoner of war. Anyone who had access to information from or about John Howard tended to believe that gaolers should be salaried, that classification should be implemented, and that silent solitary confinement was the most effective way to reform prisons and prisoners.

A bas relief of John Howard greets visitors at Wormwood Scrubbs, an old prison in London. Along with a similar bas relief of Elizabeth Fry (see below), it communicates an important message—that the institution was based on the humanitarian principles Howard exemplified. The same can be said of correctional education, especially when we consider its historic roots.

The chaplaincy is the root of the earliest institutional programming, including correctional education. Only chaplains cared enough about the welfare of convicts to implement institutional programs. Typically, this concern was expressed through a desire to help convicts acquire literacy, so they could read the Bible and be "saved" for Christ.

Robert Raikes acted on this motivation in 1781 when he started what became the international Sunday school movement. Raikes was a religious tutor at Bridewell, a famous English gaol. He decided that literacy was connected to humanitarian Christian aspirations, so he began to apply "outside" what he had learned to do "inside." The result was the Sunday school movement, which flourished as a massive, worldwide enterprise during the next six or seven decades. Europeans established Sunday schools wherever they went—during an age of imperialism when they went almost everywhere. It has been one strategy in the effort to Westernize the population worldwide.

The gaol at which Raikes worked, Bridewell, was famous because it had an industry. Convicts made tennis balls for the wealthy. The idea of a gaol with an industry was replicated in several locations, and various industries were implemented. The word "bridewell" has come to mean a gaol with a work program, instead of designating only the particular Bridewell institution where the model was established and tested.

"Inside," Sunday schools were called Sabbath schools. Cell study was the original Sabbath school model for moral and religious instruction. Many correctional educators are familiar with the cell study model, mostly from applications in segregated housing units (SHUs) and other forms of solitary confinement. Sabbath schools flourished in solitary confinement prisons, implemented according to Howard's recommendation. This type of prison was managed through a regime that came to be known as the Pennsylvania system of prison management.

Quakers in Philadelphia were anxious about the torture, fines, and mutilation that were meted out legally as colonial America's response to crime. To correct this situation they sought to establish a prison, which was eventually constructed in 1773 on Walnut Street—hence the name by which we know the institution: Walnut Street Jail. In the United States, despite the fact that several prisons predated it, this facility is known as the "cradle of the penitentiary."

The Philadelphia Society for Alleviating the Miseries of Public Prisons was founded soon thereafter, in recognition that the Walnut Street Jail might actually have caused more problems than it solved. The Society decided that education was an appropriate vehicle to address many of those problems. Therefore, clergyman William Rogers, a Society member, embarked on an educational experiment.

In 1787, with the warden's permission, Rogers gathered convicts into a large room for instruction. The warden was tense about the experiment. He thought it might result in a riot, so he required that an armed group of guards be present in the room, with a loaded cannon filled with grapeshot, aimed directly at the students. Despite this intrusion the project was a great success. It opened the door to congregate classrooms (an alternative to cell study). During the American Revolution Walnut Street Jail was used to confine Tories (Americans who sided with the British). In 1793 the Jail became a State prison.

Without express approval to establish a classroom, from a typically reluctant warden, the only way to implement school programs in a Pennsylvania system institution was through cell study—an extremely individualized approach. If you want to imagine what a Sabbath school was like, consider the following:

a. Instruction was only offered on the Sabbath (Sunday), by the chaplain. Very rarely did anyone else care enough about the improvement of convicts to provide instructional services. The rationale for the Sabbath school was consistent with America's Protestant roots. Only literate prisoners could read the Bible for themselves and be saved for Christ.

b. The chaplain was generally a volunteer. His income was earned through work with his congregation(s) in the outside community. Therefore, Sabbath school was only in session on Sunday, and only after the pastor had completed his other duties. Typically, chaplains never got to the institution until after it was dark.

c. The lack of adequate lighting was a major problem. The only lamps were in the corridor. If a lamp was placed every 25 feet, and each cell was a few feet wide, the lamp was almost always at an oblique angle from any particular cell door. No lamps were in the cells. Each cell had an iron door and an oaken door, with a small opening to pass through food. In other words, the only light in a cell entered from a distant lamp, through a small opening, and the chaplain had to stand between the opening and the lamp to talk with the convict.

d. The Bible was the only text allowed. All other texts were contraband. Often the Bibles were printed on cheap, thin paper that rotted quickly in the damp prisons. The print was very small, and this compounded the difficulties of seeing during the dark evening hours.

e. Time was a problem, because the chaplain had so many non-education responsibilities. Early surveys indicated that 5.5 to 7.0 minutes/convict/week was considered the requirement for a successful learning program. The Sabbath school model of moral and religious instruction did not provide timely reinforcement of learning.

It is often assumed that this model remained unchanged throughout the 1787-1875 period, but this view is not confirmed by the historical record. It is known as the Sabbath school period, and it was a time of gradual development in correctional education. The Sabbath school concept was dynamic. First, permission from the warden was required, because talking was against the rules but instruction requires dialogue. Second, church volunteers (often seminary students) were solicited as volunteer teachers. Finally, a movement toward salaried, full-time chaplains gained popularity. The accoutrements of traditional schools were gradually acquired—benches, slates and maps, small libraries, and secular texts.

Sabbath schools did not have norm- or criterion-referenced tests of achievement or for the diagnosis of learning needs The concept of discrete grade levels would only develop in the subsequent decades. Instead, schools reported progress in traditional measures that were similar to what modern whole language reading teachers call "bench marks." Students were diagnosed, and their progress was monitored, according to practical standards. How many students could write their names? How many knew numbers? The letters of the alphabet? How many could read but not write? How many could read and write?

The first full-time resident chaplain was Jared Curtis. He was also the first person to bring seminary students into the institution as teachers, and implemented the first statistical needs assessment of identified student learning needs. Curtis worked at Auburn Prison, in New York State, but his salary was provided by the Massachusetts Prison Discipline Society.

The Philadelphia prison that replaced the one on Walnut Street was also named for its location, Cherry Hill. It later became known as Eastern Penitentiary, opened in 1829. This prison had radial wings around a central control hub, a design which was popular for decades because it increased the effectiveness of supervision. A few guards at the hub could see down all the corridors to survey the convicts at a glance.

<u>Early Influence of the Pennsylvania System</u>

Another Pennsylvania system prison was opened in 1827, in Pittsburgh, called Western Penitentiary. Compared to today's cells, Pennsylvania system prisons had relatively spacious cells. When an inmate lived and worked in the same cell, more room was required than today, when inmates live in a cell or a dormitory and work or participate in programs in another area. This space requirement contributed to the high cost per inmate at the Eastern and Western penitentiaries.

The Pennsylvania system was little more than solitary confinement, with a Bible and a brief weekly visit from the chaplain. Some of the early penitentiaries had cell doors so short that a person had to kneel down to enter—thereby preparing the convicts for the prescribed posture of prayer. The whole design was based on the highest ideal, and on John Howard's state-of-the-art recommendations. Nevertheless, boredom was a terrible problem.

The State sought to earn money from convict labor, to defray the expense of incarceration. Cottage industries were established, such as making hosiery, brooms, furniture, and shoes or boots. Cells frequently had spinning wheels or looms. The cottage industry system relied on separate, individual workers to whom an entrepreneur brought raw materials and took away the finished products. Benches and other furniture in the cells were made with hinges, so they could be folded up against the wall at night, when the bed was folded down.

The cottage industry system was used because a factory system would have required the convicts to gather in workshops, contrary to the Pennsylvania understanding of John Howard's recommendation for separation. Factory labor was inconsistent with the Pennsylvania system of solitary confinement because factories are congregate (not separate) shops. Industries in Pennsylvania system prisons tended to have marginal profitability because the cottage system was relatively inefficient. The result was that prisons were relatively expensive. Cottage industry profits did not completely defray the high costs of confinement, as opposed to factory models, which actually made money.

Quakers on both sides of the Atlantic, in America and England, were in close communication regarding the perceived benefits of the Pennsylvania system. Many Quakers sought to establish a direct link between the Pennsylvania system and Howard's recommendation, as a tangible way to reform prisons. Thomas Eddy was a New York Quaker who petitioned the State legislature to construct a Pennsylvania system prison. Eventually he succeeded. Newgate Prison, named after a prison in London, was established in 1797.

Newgate was located in New York City's Greenwich Village, a rural setting at that time. Eddy was appointed warden, but the Legislature was skeptical about his recommendation to apply the Pennsylvania system. Instead of giving Eddy full reign, the legislature required that an experiment must be implemented to determine whether the Pennsylvania system could live up to the claims of its supporters.

The Newgate convicts were divided into three groups. The first group had no programs at all. The second group was managed according to the Pennsylvania system, with silence, cottage industries, and cell study. The third group slept in solitary cells, but were assigned to work in congregate, silent shops during the day; no talking was allowed.

Newgate was closed in 1816, and the third part of the experiment (solitary cells at night, silent work in congregate shops during the day) was declared successful. It was successful in part because it was financially lucrative. The new system was supposed to be consistent with John Howard's recommendation, since the silence rule would prevent contamination by crime. Its success in the Newgate experiment marked the first major damage to the reputation of the Pennsylvania system.

The second round of damage was administered by an important English author. In 1842, Charles Dickens visited Eastern Penitentiary, Philadelphia's Solitary Prison. The report appeared as a chapter of his book *American Notes*. Dickens found that the staff was cooperative and forthright, and that they appeared to have the highest aims. Nevertheless, the Pennsylvania system, with its lack of human contact, made prisoners insane.

Dickens wrote that each prisoner was led to, and when his sentence ended, from his solitary cell in a black hood or shroud so he could not identify the location of his cell. There were only determinate sentences then, and they were very rigid. So prisoners watched the seasons change, and grew old, in their single cell. Dickens noticed that they all blushed when he visited because they had not seen outsiders in so long and were embarrassed at the sight of a stranger. Some lost their hearing because there was nothing to hear.

Dickens wrote that when the men were released they acted like they were drunk: disoriented and unaccustomed to using their legs. He maintained that he could identify anyone who was recently released from that prison, even if the person was in a crowded room full of "normal people." Dickens proclaimed emphatically that the Pennsylvania system, despite its high, reform-oriented aims and its consistency with John Howard's recommendations, caused more problems than it helped to correct.

Nevertheless, the Pennsylvania system is still alive and well today. We call it solitary confinement, in all its various forms. And it survived long after Dickens' whistle-blowing public relations effort. By 1854 the Pennsylvania system was officially eliminated in America. However, it lived on for decades in Europe, and especially in Dickens' own England. The reason is largely attributable to a single woman, Elizabeth Fry.

Elizabeth Fry, Literacy, and the Pennsylvania System

Of the two bas reliefs at London's Wormwood Scrubbs Prison, one portrayed John Howard, and the other Elizabeth Fry. She was an English Quaker who advocated correctional education and the Pennsylvania system as a full-time, voluntary career. Through her steadfast labor the Pennsylvania system was implemented in prisons all over Great Britain and Europe.

Fry began her correctional education work around the outskirts of the great Metropolis of London, teaching poor people how to read. In 1809 she began organizing literacy and work programs at London's Newgate Prison. Fry was known especially for distributing Bibles and attending to the education and work-oriented needs of confined women, and, often, their children.

Based on her sisters' biography of Elizabeth Fry, the present authors constructed a single-spaced, typed list of her major contacts, her advocacy network. It was restricted to heads of state, prime ministers, and royalty of various nations. The list spanned three pages, and included VIPs from

Scandinavia to the Mediterranean; from England to Russia. These were only people with whom she visited and corresponded regularly. She also had many intermittent contacts. Elizabeth Fry was a one person social advocacy movement, organizing, lobbying, and speaking wherever she went—and she traveled a great deal. Her husband was a relatively wealthy businessman during most of their life together, and Fry was well connected. Wherever she went people got excited about the perceived benefits of the Pennsylvania system and correctional education. She organized the London Prison Discipline Society, which became important linchpin to subsequent parts of this history.

It is interesting to note that Sarah Martin, known as "the prisoners' friend," embarked on a correctional education career at England's Great Yarmouth Gaol at approximately the same time as Elizabeth Fry. However, because she was poor and not well prepared for professional networking, Martin was unable to improve educational opportunities beyond the gaol in which she worked. She wrote that prisoner students possessed vast learning needs, but they were basically cooperative, friendly, and supportive of learning. The real problem, she wrote, was the prison administration and guards, and their attitude toward prison education.

One part of Fry's agenda was the adoption of the Pennsylvania system in the United Kingdom and Europe. As a result, the Pennsylvania system was retained there long after it had been discredited in America. This required various adaptations and refinements because, despite the good sentiments of all those around her, the system was inherently deficient. The Pennsylvania system was retained in Europe long after it should have been replaced.

There was a particular problem associated with women offenders. This was a time when women were considered the major civilizing influence in society. If a man committed a crime, it was not that significant as he was just one step above being a barbarian. However, if a woman did so, she fell so far from her natural state, and off the pedestal established by the culture, that she was, literally, a "fallen angel." (Freedman, 1981). Treatment for women prisoners was called by Lewis a "sexual double standard," especially if the woman was convicted of a sexual crime (1965, p.157). In addition there were so few women prisoners compared to men (around five percent of the population), that it seemed unnecessarily expensive to have separate facilities for women. At first women prisoners were housed in a wing of the male prison. But the prison reform systems were generally not applied to the women. The Auburn prison had a women's wing, but during the 1820s there was no separate cell for them, they all served their time in a one-room attic (Freedman, 1981, p. 15). It was extremely difficult for separate institutions to be built, as the women also provided the cooking and cleaning for the male prison.

A problem accrued from the difficulties in getting physical exercise in a solitary system, while attempting to maintain separate system ideals. In one English prison group exercise was established on a separate basis. Each man marched while grasping a rope and wearing a visor through which only the back of the neck of the man directly in front of him was visible. If the rows of men were straight, the rope they each held would also be straight, so the guard could easily survey the situation. This procedure ensured that Howard's recommendation to separate the convicts would be implemented, with no breach of security.

In one English adaptation of the Pennsylvania system, little cubicles like telephone booths were constructed to allow a large group of men to attend lectures such as, "the evils of alcoholism." At another prison a similar system of booths was constructed to accommodate "congregate" church services while consistent with Howard's "separate" recommendation. In both situations the tiny, individual booths inhibited communication and cut off the other prisoners from view. The chaplain and the guard could see and be seen by each prisoner, but the prisoners could not see each other.

About this time English philosopher Jeremy Bentham introduced the Panopticon design, a round prison. It was more efficient than the Cherry Hill design, with its radial arms or wings. The Panopticon design was later implemented at Stateville, in Illinois. Cherry Hill's radial design and Bentham's Panopticon design functioned like the little booths, making prisoners visible to their keepers but not to each other. They also maximized the efficiency of surveillance by a small staff of keepers. Most cost-cutting efforts have traditionally hinged on the reduction of required staff positions. This is an important factor today in the design of entrepreneurial or contract prisons—in the privatization of corrections.

The Auburn System and the Pilsbury Dynasty

In 1825, after closing Newgate Prison, New York State opened Auburn Prison. Auburn had been established under the same State law that created Newgate, and housed many of its inmates. Auburn was managed according to the silent system, the third plan that was piloted at Newgate. Eventually, the silent system became known as the Auburn system. It was widely adopted, and eventually replaced the Pennsylvania system in prisons throughout the United States.

The Auburn system of prison discipline consisted of solitary confinement in separate cells at night, and work in congregate shops under the silence rule during the day. This routine was said to be consistent with Howard's recommendations. Auburn was an exceptionally repressive (coercive/manipulative) system because it was so regimented.

Convicts were marched in lockstep from their cells each morning to deposit their toilet bucket waste in the sewer. From there they were marched on to work for a few hours. Then they were marched to breakfast, to work, to lunch, to work, to dinner, and back to their cells. The lockstep procedure increased guard surveillance capability. It accomplished this by making sure everyone was in place. In lockstep men were required to look at their toes, with their right hand on the shoulder of the next man in front. Chewing gum or tobacco was forbidden because guards had a difficult time identifying whether a man was chewing or talking. This is the origin of the modern public school rule that outlaws gum, even though many believe it accrued from the mess made by used gum. Eventually, the requirement that each man put his hand on the shoulder of the next man was abandoned, for fear that the contact fostered homosexuality. Instead, they crossed their arms on their chests, holding their own shoulders.

Auburn inmates complained that "the Big Eye" was always upon them. Constant surveillance was a major program component, a point of departure between the Auburn and Pennsylvania systems. How much wrong could a man do in a Pennsylvania solitary cell? In one of his 1922 Yale University lectures, prison reformer Thomas Mott Osborne proposed that the Pennsylvania system was established to make men "think" right, and the Auburn system was established to make men "act" right. There was a strong link between Auburn and the behavioral psychology that emerged in the 19th century.

Auburn system prisons had factories, called congregate workshops. Again, factories are more efficient economically than cottage industries. This meant that Auburn system prisons could out-produce Pennsylvania system prisons, thereby reducing the expense of incarceration—sometimes they even made a profit. Legislators liked factory prisons because they actually contributed to state treasuries. With factories inside the walls, legislators could avoid or diminish the need to raise taxes regularly. This enhanced the ability of incumbents to be re-elected. Prisons, politics, and the economy resulted in the proliferation of the Auburn system.

The benefits of that system came to be closely associated with Amos Pilsbury, the greatest Auburn champion of the 19th century. The "Pilsbury dynasty" was a vast political machine, with formal authority and informal influence in prisons throughout what we now call the Northeast, the region in which most early American prisons were located. Moses Pilsbury founded the dynasty; it was carried on by Amos (Moses' son), and Louis (Moses' grandson).

The Pilsburys hired, fired, and promoted freely, in accord with dynastic needs. Relatives and friends ascended the career ladder; others were locked into low level jobs or terminated. If you were a clerk and the Pilsburys liked you, quick promotion to deputy warden or warden was possible. The dynasty was so powerful that if they wanted to promote you but no suitable assignment was available, they would have a new prison constructed so you could have an important job. Pilsbury authority accrued directly from legislative support for the Auburn system.

Moses was warden in New Hampshire, then at Connecticut's Wethersfield Prison, then he moved to New York State. Wethersfield, opened in 1827, was a showcase institution. It replaced the Simsbury Mines Prison, fashioned from an old copper mine. Like the Walnut Street Jail, Simsbury had been used to confine Tories during the American Revolution. It consisted of subterranean cells, dark and without heat, into which food was periodically dropped—usually measured amounts of salt pork, bread or cornmeal, and water. Any prison that replaced the Simsbury Mines was bound to be perceived as a success, and Moses capitalized on that public relations advantage. Wethersfield was managed according to the Auburn system. From New England to Michigan, to the Middle Atlantic states, the Pilsburys had profound influence. They were good managers. The Pilsbury "machine" was the prison management Establishment.

Moses Pilsbury initiated the habit of donating $25 annually from his personal salary for prison library books at the New Hampshire Prison, where he had previously served as warden. This custom was quickly institutionalized, and became a factor in the secularization of prison library collections. Previously, religious tracts and Bibles dominated the collections. Twenty-five dollars was a lot of money during the first half of the 19th century. Pilsburys also endorsed the policy of charging a nickel to anyone from the community who wanted to come in and look at the prisoners—just as people pay to see the animals at a zoo. It became a pastime in many communities to go look at the prisoners after church on Sundays. The proceeds were supposed to support the prison library. The only problem was that many wardens did not want to spend the money on books, so it was dedicated to library funds but rarely spent. Nearly a hundred years later, when several libraries burned down, they were quickly replaced with these funds, which had amassed from huge quantities of nickels over the decades.

Louis Dwight founded the Boston Prison Discipline Society in 1825, to advocate the Auburn system. There was a hot debate at that time between partisans of the Auburn and Pennsylvania systems. The Boston Prison Discipline Society's public orientation made little mention of the economic advantages of Auburn factories over Pennsylvania cottage industries. Instead, the Society described the educational advantages of the Auburn system. It became a repository for information about correctional education, and helped many interested chaplains learn about state-of-the-art educational models that were used in various institutions around the country.

The Auburn system education advantage consisted of the capability to establish traditional, grouped classroom education, instead of cell study. If the warden agreed to waive the silence requirement for school purposes, all that was needed was a slate and chalk, some texts, benches, and a teacher. Education was an excellent low-cost strategy to keep prisoners occupied and impress the outside community with the quality of institutional programming. Correctional education was a political issue. In 1847 a New York law permitted the assignment of two guards at each prison to serve as teachers.

Despite the forces gathering to support correctional education, there was still much resistance. In 1824, the Auburn warden resisted efforts of some local church volunteers to establish "Three Rs" education for young offenders.

The warden cited "the dangers to society of educated convicts." This attitude reflected the earlier sentiment of the Walnut Street Jail loaded cannon procedure. The 1847 New York correctional teacher law was not operationalized for years—some wardens quietly refused to implement the mandate. This anti-education sentiment is still with us. For example, in the mid-1980s a report from a western U.S. state indicated that the new Corrections Commissioner called all the wardens together to tell them, "You can have inmates, or you can have books (libraries), but you can't have both inmates and books."

Similarly, Moses Pilsbury supported prison libraries; later wardens carried on his tradition but would not spend the money on library books. These examples suggest that spirit of the Auburn system, and the systems that succeeded it, may have been more lasting than any of its specific attributes. That is the central dynamic of institutionalization—the loss of a system's original, humanistic rationale, while retaining its rules and procedures.

Wardens during this period did not speak with inmates. If an inmate had something to say, he told it to a guard, who told the principal keeper, who told the warden. The Pilsburys had clubs, knives, and pistols strapped to their bodies, because they were fearful of enraged or desperate convicts. When Amos Pilsbury died, his last gasped and strained words announced that he was sorry he had advocated the Auburn system so successfully—that the prisons were worse than they had been under the Pennsylvania system, despite the good intentions of Auburn advocates. Blake McKelvey wrote a book entitled *American Prisons: A History of Good Intentions* (1977). This title is both descriptive and accurate; it tells the story of the Pennsylvania and Auburn systems. Like the inmates in their prisons, these systems were victims of institutionalization.

State governments were not the only players in this grand drama. City governments applied great effort to keep juvenile delinquents off the street. The New York City rendition, in the late decades of the 19th century, was carried out by Tammany Hall, but the same dynamic was present in all large American cities. Roving bands of youngsters wreaked havoc on pedestrians, shopkeepers, and peddlers. A new social institution had to be established to constrain these delinquents. Reform schools and compulsory school attendance laws were designed, in part, to accomplish that aim.

Reform schools, with mandatory attendance, were managed with control as the guiding principle. Teachers' desks were elevated, so students had to look up to address their betters, thereby lending the status of authority. An emphasis on decorum and rote memory prevailed. The term "toe the line" referred to an actual procedure, in which students would walk right up to a line drawn on the floor before reciting for the teacher's review. Reform schools were managed like junior prisons. There was a heavy work orientation, sometimes labeled vocational training.

On the whole, control—not learning or growth—was the focus of reform schools. Eventually, these models were studied by urban school reformers. Many of the procedures that were piloted in reform schools, and later in reformatories for young adults, were applied to local schools in the free community. Of special interest were the reform school approaches to vocational education, military education, and physical education, as well as a general tendency to individualize services and records, which were borrowed extensively by the leaders of emerging urban school districts. The development of compulsory attendance in local schools meant students were off the street for at least six hours. This procedure first emerged in residential reform schools.

Maconochie and the Emergence of Reformatory Prison Discipline

Captain Alexander Maconochie conceived and implemented a third system for managing prisons (in addition to the Pennsylvania and Auburn systems), called Reformatory Prison Discipline. This system ultimately replaced the other two, with the exception of some remnants today. Maconochie's programs in the 1840s were prototypic models that set the pace for all subsequent corrections procedures. They included the first modern examples of systematic classification, progressive housing, indeterminate sentences, and parole; in addition, Maconochie experimented with adult and vocational education. He was the founder of most modern corrections efforts.

Alexander Maconochie was a Scot, distantly related to the economist Adam Smith. He was a captain in Her Majesty's Navy, and a veteran of the Napoleonic wars. He fought against America in the War of 1812. Like John Howard, Maconochie had been a prisoner of war, held captive by the French.

Maconochie was a geographer. He was the first geographer to be admitted to the Royal Scientific Academy, and is noted as the first geography professor in Scotland. During this period, the South Pacific was the world's great geographic frontier, and Captain Maconochie longed to see it first hand.

Australia was a cluster of six British penal colonies at the time. It had taken the British about 20 years after the American Revolution to realize that they could transport (exile) their criminals to Australia, to relieve the overcrowded hulk prisons. Penal colonies developed in Australia because there was a decision to avoid building new prisons in the United Kingdom, and the American market was closed off.

Colonel George Arthur was a brutal Australian governor (head warden)—in fact, his whole system of prison management can be summarized in the single word "brutality." Arthur had implemented a vast system of slave labor, convict spies, and horrific torture. When Arthur was reassigned to Upper Canada, Maconochie's friend Lord Franklin became the new Australian governor. Franklin invited Maconochie to come to the South Pacific with him, and Maconochie accepted the challenge. Since Franklin had no idea about the penal colony staffing structure, he offered to make Maconochie his personal secretary until a better job could be identified for him in Australia.

Before Maconochie left the London Prison Discipline Society, the organization that Elizabeth Fry had founded, asked him to write periodic reports on the state of transported felons. There was a lot of interest in transportation, especially in reform-minded community organizations that had heard of the many abuses. With Lord Franklin's permission, Maconochie agreed to send the reports.

The Franklin/Maconochie team arrived in Australia in 1837. Maconochie was appalled at the enormity of the abuse that he saw. As in America, the labor shortage was intense. Convicts were sold as slaves to free settlers who cared little for the well being of their charges. Flogging was an everyday event; men were chained to rocks at the beach for punishment, so they would have to stretch and strain to breath when the tide came in; sexual abuses were the norm. These horrors were beyond the scope of what Maconochie could accept. He expressed himself diplomatically, proposed an alternative management scheme, and ran into trouble with the remnants of Colonel Arthur's old staff.

Eleven-year-old pickpockets were being transported to Australia, as a substitute for hanging. Over 200 crimes resulted in death sentences, which were frequently commuted to transportation, acts of "mercy" by the king. The London Prison Discipline Society launched an anti-transportation campaign and used Maconochie's reports, for purposes to which he had never agreed. The reports were entered as papers of Parliament, the English equivalent of the *Congressional Record*. Some were published on the front pages of London newspapers, while their author, Maconochie, was two years away and unable to offer any explanation. The Government was embarrassed, and Maconochie became the scapegoat. Even the prime minister was shamefaced about the honest content of Maconochie's remarks. It made no difference that Lord Franklin, even the Home Secretary in the Prime Minister's Cabinet, had reviewed the reports in advance and given Maconochie permission to submit them to the Society. Franklin was instructed by the Home Office to fire Maconochie.

Maconochie, unemployed in the city of Hobartown in Van Dieman's Land (Tasmania), used his free time to write books about how to improve the Australian prison system he had encountered and studied. Knowledgeable about both the Pennsylvania and Auburn systems, he rejected both. Instead, he wrote how to implement a humane prison system, capable of reforming prisoners. Maconochie's whole prison reform career was rooted in the aspiration that correction could be accomplished without brutality. Part of the problem, he wrote, was that the system was bad for the people who controlled convicts, as well as for the convicts themselves. He called his alternate plan the Mark System because it was based on a behaviorally-oriented process in which officers awarded marks for good behavior in record books. Today we know the Mark System by another name, Reformatory Prison Discipline.

Meanwhile, in London the political climate had changed again. To show support for a potentially reformed transportation system, the Home Office now wanted to exalt Maconochie. He was rehired, this time, to be the warden of

Norfolk Island penal colony. Maconochie arrived there shortly before Queen Victoria's birthday, in May, 1840. By this time, his complete Reformatory Prison Discipline System plan was ready to be operationalized.

Norfolk Island was a very secure, maximum security prison colony, about 800 miles off the Australian coast. Only "doubly convicted felons" were sent there, men who had been transported to Australia and then committed a crime at a penal colony.

The term "ringleader" was coined at Norfolk Island. The large lumber yard was arranged like a circle or ring. Before Maconochie's tenure at Norfolk, convicts were in charge inside the ring—gambling, illegal alcohol, and homosexuality were the rule. Officers who went inside the ring were summarily murdered. Outside the ring, officers were in charge. The Norfolk Island facility had such an abhorrently brutal regime that felons frequently made sham attempts to kill officers for the sole purpose of getting condemned to hang. Death was considered preferable to the completion of a long sentence. Norfolk Island was considered one of the worst prisons.

Soon after he arrived there as warden, Maconochie ordered that the prison house doors be opened and the convicts released. He called them all to a meeting, and informed them that he had a plan for improving the penal colony. However, the plan required that they must live up to their responsibilities as good community members.

To demonstrate that he thought they could be trusted, Maconochie said they would be freed for the entire day. He would provide food and supplies for a fantastic patriotic celebration in honor of Queen Victoria's birthday. The only requirement was that they return to their cells by 7:00 that evening. If they could not do this, he would assume that they were not interested in changing the existing system. The convicts agreed to these terms. After a 21 gun salute to Victoria, Maconochie had the staff dispense the best provisions for a great picnic feast, along with rum for a patriotic toast to the Queen. He arranged fireworks displays, and the men organized spontaneous choral and dramatic events. The day was a wonderful success, and all the men returned to their cells before 7:00 that night. By the appointed hour the officers said they could hear a pin drop. Maconochie had made his point. The convicts proved that they could live up to the trust he put in them.

His decision to celebrate a patriotic event was another in the long series of brilliant initiatives credited to Maconochie. The anti-patriotic sentiment of modern inmates was similar to that experienced by Norfolk's doubly convicted felons, who blamed the government for their confinement. Indeed, each had been originally transported to Australia by a special royal order of mercy—a pardon from death by hanging. Many, particularly the Irish, considered themselves political prisoners. By linking his reforms with the national celebration of Queen Victoria's birthday, Maconochie helped the men re-evaluate their relationship with the government, and with the society it represented.

(There is an interesting aside about all this that relates indirectly to one of the current authors, Thom Gehring. One of the convicts who was unloaded in the First Fleet of transported felons to Botany Bay was one Thomas Gearing. He was convicted for stealing plate from the chapel of Magdelan College, at Oxford University, and subsequently transported by the mercy of the King George. Another report attributes Gearing's incarceration to pickpocketing; perhaps both are true. Gearing died at sea on his way to Botany Bay. As it happened, the First Fleet arrived in Australia on the current author's birthday, January 26, in the year 1788.)

As soon as the free settlers on the Australian mainland heard of Maconochie's phenomenal success at Norfolk Island they pressured the Home Office, and Maconochie was fired again. However, it took until 1842 for him to get news of his termination. The letter that informed him of dismissal was full of praise for his foresight and good planning. Then it took two years to find a substitute warden and get him to Australia, so Maconochie did not leave his post until 1844.

During the 1840-44 period, Maconochie operationalized the procedural foundations of modern corrections. First he implemented John Howard's classification recommendation, to make sure that hardened criminals were not grouped together with the few who were still relatively new to crime. Then he organized the convicts into groups of six, and instructed each group that marks would be awarded on a group basis, rather than for individuals. This procedure was used until the group earned a minimal requirement of marks. Positive peer pressure helped change the Norfolk milieu.

After the critical number of good conduct marks was earned by a group, in proportion to marks amassed by individuals, each convict was allowed proportional privileges and better housing. When a fixed number of marks had been earned, a ticket of leave (parole) was awarded. Through this procedure, Maconochie officially discarded with fixed sentences. Instead, the indeterminate sentence emerged. Corrections and correctional education have never been the same since his auspicious tenure at Norfolk Island.

Reformatory Prison Discipline was designed to reform, and it worked. If a man continued to act like a criminal, marks were not earned, and he remained in prison. If he showed evidence of reform, he was seen to be a good risk—probably able to resist the temptation to commit crime—and was released under supervision. The plan allowed men to fail or succeed, and permitted opportunities for individual decision-making. If a man failed, the system itself was not threatened with chaos. Instead, the man simply did not get treated as well and stayed "inside" longer. It took courage for Maconochie and the staff to let men have enough freedom so they could make decisions, knowing that some would decide to fail (or not decide to change their lives). Maconochie decided administratively to avoid controlling everything, so the men could exert some personal responsibility for their own behavior.

Much modern sentiment is directed against indeterminate sentencing procedures. On the whole, this sentiment results from the arbitrary way in which many subsequent systems implemented indeterminate sentences. Maconochie's rationale for establishing the Mark System and tickets of leave focused on helping incarcerates prepare for life in the free community. It was not about imposing long sentences, or psychologically manipulating individuals into capitulation. Each generation of corrections managers who implemented indeterminate sentences gradually forgot more and more of Maconochie's original rationale, and replaced it with their own interest in controlling everything in the institution. From this perspective, the emphasis on inmate responsibility (and on the ability to fail as well as succeed) was anathema to good institutional management. In essence, Reformatory Prison Discipline was institutionalized in the United States by employees who had worked in coercive Auburn system institutions. In Maconochie's time, the indeterminate sentence was new, vital, and reform-oriented. Modern efforts retain just parts of the innovative system.

Maconochie encouraged religious observances, fostered reading, established an inmate police squad, allowed headstones on convict graves, and let interested men witness hearings for disciplinary infractions. Attendance at the hearings was important because it let everyone see that his fair procedures were uniformly applied. As warden, Maconochie talked with convicts. This was an unprecedented innovation. He built a gaol (for solitary confinement—punishment) that opened up to the chapel, and he awarded extra marks to convicts who read aloud to the men assigned there. He let convicts grow their own private gardens to ensure a healthful diet, and established a market economy to permit private sale of any surplus of which they wanted to dispose. Maconochie started an agricultural school. While he was warden, the ring (lumber yard) was dismantled. He established a band and a system of music instruction.

Captain Bligh, of Mutiny on the Bounty infamy, followed soon after Maconochie's immediate successor. That gives an idea of the reversal Norfolk Island experienced after Maconochie's departure. Brutality and the ring were reinstated. Years later Maconochie testified before Parliament about transportation and his Reformatory Prison Discipline System. He described how few officers were actually required to maintain order during the 1840-44 period, and how they were able to discard the traditional, harsh procedures, to adopt a more helpful role in the lives of convicts. Reformatory Prison Discipline had succeeded in transforming the prison colony into a school, and the British Navy guards who functioned as correctional officers into teachers. Education was a hallmark of the colony's programs.

Maconochie returned to England and became allied with a political reformer named Matthew Davenport Hill. The two worked well together, and Maconochie told Hill all about his exciting experiment on Norfolk Island. Hill was a recorder, a type of judge with some influence, and he managed to get Maconochie appointed warden of the Birmingham, England Prison. This assignment lasted only two years, from 1849-1851, and it was very frustrating for him. The Birmingham Prison Board of Managers would not let Maconochie implement his proven methods. Instead, he was forced to manage a traditional prison, complete with a treadmill (device for providing hard labor that produced no product) and other assorted instruments and procedures of punishment and brutality. Maconochie died a few years later, sadly convinced that his tested design would die with him. However, a remarkable chain of international events led to exactly the opposite result—the application of his Reformatory Prison Discipline design in several nations.

American Interest in Maconochie's Reformatory Prison Discipline

Meanwhile in the United States, the Auburn system was flourishing. The lockstep, striped uniforms, and extreme regimentation dominated what many now call the corrections industry. The Pilsburys had consolidated their power.

Zebulon Brockway began as a clerk in 1848 at Connecticut's Wethersfield Prison. Brockway listened as the old staff told stories about Amos Pilsbury, who had left Wethersfield as warden several years before. Although Brockway had never met Pilsbury, he came to admire the former warden. Consistent with past practice in the dynasty, Pilsbury's brother-in-law Leonard Wells had succeeded Amos as the Wethersfield warden, and the place was alive with the telling and retelling of Amos' success.

Through Wells, Pilsbury eventually heard of Brockway's admiration, and had him reassigned to another institution as deputy warden. Brockway was only 24. This began Brockway's administrative career. Soon he acquired a reputation as a warden of showcase institutions controlled by the Pilsburys—first in New York State, then in Connecticut, then in New York again, then in Michigan, and finally back in New York. Despite his meteoric rise through Pilsbury influence, Brockway was part of the first generation of professional prison managers who came up through the ranks, rather than rich men who merely dabbled in institutional work.

His role as Pilsbury's warden of showcase institutions resulted in Brockway managing the Detroit House of Correction. It was one of the most advanced facilities in the nation, with an indeterminate sentencing procedure that came close to Maconochie's model. While in Detroit, Brockway visited a juvenile institution for females in Lancaster, Massachusetts. He believed females deserved separate facilities, so he constructed a female annex to the Detroit House of Correction, and named it the Detroit House of Shelter. He hired Emma Hall and other teachers. Hall had been a Detroit elementary school teacher; Brockway hired her as a matron.

The abuses prevalent in female wings of male prisons were legendary. Prisoners often became pregnant by the officer staff. One step was to have females serve as matrons to protect the prisoners. The next step was to have separate facilities built for women prisoners, managed by women matrons.

Even when these were developed, however, programs for women lagged far behind those for men.

Like the Detroit House of Correction, the Detroit House of Shelter soon became a famous as a prototypic model program, and Emma Hall's fame increased proportionally. She established a social education program for women, designed to help them transition back into society. The Detroit House of Shelter is considered the first reformatory for women in the United States, and an improvement over the earlier system of housing women in the same building with the men. Later, when Brockway left Detroit, Hall became a local superintendent of schools.

Enoch Wines was the intellectual of the Pilsbury prison management group. Wines was general secretary of the New York Prison Association, the successor organization to the Boston Prison Discipline Society. Brockway and Wines worked together on projects that the Pilsburys identified as important to fledgling prison systems. They helped outline the future of the emerging corrections industry.

Wines' studies of prisons and juvenile institutions suggested that the Auburn system, although championed by the Pilsburys, was flawed. New procedures were needed to monitor inmate behavior and to release those inmates whose behavior indicated they might be a good risk for release. The Pilsbury group needed to improve on the Detroit House of Correction program—they needed a rationale and integrated program for accomplishing what Maconochie had accomplished in the South Pacific. Instead, they floundered because of strident legislative support for the revenue producing Auburn system. But from time to time they got news of a better system, in Ireland.

At international prison discipline conferences Sir Walter Crofton, Ireland's exemplary prison manager, announced that he had not flogged a man in three years, thanks to his implementation of Maconochie's system of monitoring and rewarding the good behavior of convicts. Crofton was in charge of all the prisons in Ireland during the Great Potato Famine era.

Enoch Wines eventually heard these stories about Crofton's success, which matched precisely the needs he had identified for the developing American prison systems. In 1863, he sent Sing Sing warden Gaylord Hubbell to obtain first hand information. Hubbell learned that Crofton was implementing Maconochie's Reformatory Prison Discipline System, about which he had learned from Maconochie's old friend, Matthew Davenport Hill. Although Maconochie had died several years before, Crofton implemented and extended his Norfolk Island procedures throughout the Irish prison system. Irish prisons were exploding as a result of the Potato Famine. Poor food and conditions were better than the alternative on the outside, so prison was considered an option.

Crofton even described himself as Maconochie's disciple. Reformatory Prison Discipline, which had been established in the South Pacific, was at last secure, in Ireland. The bias that England held against Ireland prevented the success of the Irish System from being widely recognized, as it was thought that the English were superior in all things. Once Wines and his Pilsbury supporters found out about the success, they wanted to implement it in the United States.

Mary Carpenter, a reformer in the tradition of Matthew Davenport Hill whose previous efforts had emphasized the need for reformatory schools and ragged schools for the children of the dangerous and perishing classes, was asked to write a report describing the implementation of Maconochie's system in Ireland. She prepared the definitive book on Crofton's exemplary nationwide corrections system. The Pilsbury group now had state-of-the-art information about how to improve the despicable Auburn system they had to helped spawn. They would apply Crofton's version of Maconochie's better idea—Reformatory Prison Discipline.

Yet how could the Pilsburys advocate any system other than Auburn? Because of Pilsbury advocacy, the state legislatures supported the Auburn System so strongly that they did not even want to discuss an alternative system. After all, it was Auburn System factories that helped them maintain low taxes and get re-elected.

Amos Pilsbury, Enoch Wines, and Zebulon Brockway conspired to hold a great conference, to disseminate the information they had obtained about Crofton's system and demonstrate support for conversion from the Auburn system to the Reformatory Prison Discipline System. That conference took place in 1870, in Cincinnati, Ohio. Judge Rutherford B. Hayes, who later became the 19th U.S. president, chaired the conference. About 130 people attended—it was a huge conference by 19th century standards. They were wardens, judges, and charity people. This gathering is known as "the starting shot of the reformatory movement" in the United States. The participants drafted a manifesto called the Declaration of Principles, with 30 resolutions about how to improve corrections and the emerging correctional profession. Principle #10 supported correctional education:

> Education is a vital force in the reformation of fallen men and women. Its tendency is to quicken the intellect, inspire self-respect, excite to higher aims, and afford a healthful substitute for low and vicious amusements. Education is therefore, a matter of primary importance in prisons, and should be carried to the utmost extent consistent with the other purposes of such institutions. (Wines, 1871, p. 542).

This conference was the birth of the effort to professionalize corrections, and of correctional standards (published criteria to evaluate the effectiveness of institutional programs). It was the origin of the American Correctional Association (ACA—originally known as the American Prison Association). The ACA logo has an eagle, perched on a great rock, with the big numbers "1870" on the rock to commemorate the 1870 Cincinnati conference. Brockway was middle aged at the time of the Cincinnati conference. Like the other participants, he was a strong advocate of the Maconochie/Crofton plan, Reformatory Prison Discipline.

However, there was a six year lag between the 1870 conference fanfare and the actual establishment of the nation's first reformatory institution for adult males. Even the Pilsbury group grew frustrated in their effort to convince legislators of the need to progress beyond the Auburn system. In the midst of this prolonged and horribly disheartening hesitation, Brockway quit his Detroit job and went to work for a railroad. Emma Hall quit, too. What was the point of it all? Brockway knew what had to be done to improve the system, but he was not allowed to implement the needed programs.

Brockway lasted only two years with the railroad. He was financially destitute when he left that brief job, the only non-corrections period in his long career. Then Brockway received a telegram from Louis Pilsbury, asking if he would like to become the warden of a new reformatory for adult males in New York State. The next day Brockway returned the message: yes, he would be happy to serve.

Louis Pilsbury was Amos' son (Moses' grandson). Brockway later reported that Louis Pilsbury was the first statewide director of corrections in New York, and the first statewide director in the country. Louis had been working diligently with the New York State legislature to gain acceptance of Reformatory Prison Discipline System.

Brockway had been an important contributor to that work. While still warden in Detroit, New York State had hired Brockway as a consultant. His first task was to coordinate the site selection committee for the reformatory. He chose Elmira, a railroad center, with several nearby colleges, on the site of an old Union prisoner of war camp during the Civil War. Elmira is in the Fingerlakes region of the State, not far from the Pennsylvania border.

Then he wrote the draft of the proposed indeterminate sentence law. Indeterminate sentences are a requirement for reformatories, as Maconochie and Crofton had demonstrated. The whole reformatory concept rests on the possibility of early release, which cannot be accomplished in a fixed sentence milieu. Demonstrated behavioral improvement must help inmates get released sooner, thus shifting responsibility for their actions squarely onto their own shoulders.

Brockway was unpleased that only one section of the final version of the amended bill was passed by the legislature. That section stated that no prisoner could be held beyond the time that would normally be associated with the determinate or fixed sentence. In other words, early release was acceptable for good behavior, but late release for bad behavior would be legally unacceptable. Historians found that this adjustment of the Maconochie/Crofton procedure was sponsored by judges. Legislators were cautious about the new Reformatory

Prison Discipline System idea, and judges were unwilling to relinquish their sentencing authority to institutional administrators. For the rest of his career Brockway remained convinced that an absolute indeterminate sentence was the best approach.

By 1876 the preliminary steps had all been completed and Elmira Reformatory opened. That event changed the direction of correctional education, and that is why the period under consideration ends in 1875. From our historical perspective, we can pose two central questions which might not have occurred to Brockway and others on the scene: Could Reformatory Prison Discipline be implemented properly by staff who had already been institutionalized in the repressive Auburn system? Could prisoners who had been institutionalized at other facilities adapt to reformatory prison discipline conditions? Some answers to those questions, and the general development of the Elmira program, will be the focus of the next major chapter, which corresponds to Brockway's tenure as Elmira superintendent, 1876-1900. However, our attention will first be directed to some contributions that were related to the progress in North America, though their impact would not be felt immediately.

European Progress in Prison Reform and Correctional Education

Substantial processes were unfolding in Europe, though the pace was phasic and intermittent. Indeed, there was great communication between both sides of the Atlantic. Readers will recall the exemplary networking of Elizabeth Fry that spurred key decision makers to foster improvements, and how her steadfast work built on that of John Howard, who was also from England, and stood out like a beacon for other nations to see. In turn, Fry's work stimulated developments in Pennsylvania and New York State.

Adding to this trajectory was the simultaneous work of several major contributors: Mary Carpenter (based in Bristol), Matthew Davenport Hill (Birmingham), Sir Walter Crofton (an Anglo-Irishman whose career was largely in Ireland), and Alexander Maconochie (who came to Birmingham after his South Pacific career); Charles Dickens was also connected to this group. In many ways Birmingham, was really the center of this cluster of prison reform and correctional education contributors and Hill's office was a repository of relevant information and a headquarters for dissemination. Though each of these personalities was at the center of a series of important innovations, their work was really coordinated and remarkably synchronized and facilitated by Hill's informal leadership. For example, it was Hill who extended Maconochie's influence after he was fired as superintendent of the Norfolk Island penal colony. Indeed, without the protracted leadership of this group, none of the improvements made in North America, especially but not only at Elmira, would have been possible. The English group packaged up the news of reforms in juvenile facilities, adult prisons, and what we would today call alternative education for American consumption, and were in that way the source of all the subsequent reforms experienced in the United States and Canada.

The writing and advocacy skills of Hill and Carpenter were especially effective in this drama. They collected and disseminated news of substantial experiments in France, Germany, and Spain, as well as on some of the docked hulks, and on a few transport ships that conveyed criminals to Australia. However, one of the most striking and important adventures in correctional education and prison reform was taking place in Switzerland. Perhaps the cadre of English correctional education contributors did not attend to the news from Switzerland with the excitement that they did the chapters of this drama from other nations because there was a general English caution about anything associated with the French Revolution.

John Henry Pestalozzi was a Swiss devotee of Rousseau and a great advocate of the principles hailed by the French Revolution. Much of his work has been summarized as an effort to psychologize education. Another apt summary would be that he continued the groundbreaking educational work which Comenius (in Poland) and Rousseau (in Switzerland and France) had started, toward a new, developmental and naturalistic approach to teaching and learning. Like Thomas Paine, George Washington, and James Madison, Pestalozzi was awarded special, international recognition by leaders of the French Revolution. Pestalozzi strongly believed in education as an intervention strategy to help individuals and communities improve their life situation. Many have written that he was the founder of the modern teacher education movement.

Pestalozzi was a prolific writer and his books were enormously popular. His early career began with the establishment of a farm community, which became bankrupt. Later he gathered up the orphans that resulted from the intense combat that was almost continuous across Europe. This problem began with the French Revolution and extended through the Napoleanic Wars. Often there were entire villages in Switzerland where all the adults had been massacred and the orphans were left completely destitute. Pestalozzi founded orphanages and schools where he gradually refined his educational method. Eventually he prepared teachers to carry on his work. Always his approach was based on love and affection, even when faced with massive resistance from the children—there had been a long tradition of religious wars throughout Europe, and children had been raised to be exceptionally skeptical of outsiders, especially when the outsiders represented a different religion.

Despite his partisanship for the spirit of the Revolution, Pestalozzi never fared well with the Revolutionary authorities. For example, at one point the local Swiss Revolutionary government facilitated the move of one of Pestalozzi's orphanages to an old abbey that was out of use because of the war. However, they soon came back to reassume possession, transforming the facility into a much needed military hospital. At another point Pestalozzi's credibility rose as a result of the international recognition that the Paris Revolutionary government extended to him. However, when he went to Paris to advocate educational innovations to the central government, several ministers summarily rejected his message, explaining that the press of war and other improvements must come before education. In short, Pestalozzi's perceived "closeness" to the ideological action, which accrued mostly from the revolutionary dimension of his writings, never resulted in tangible, stable results that he could use to improve his program. Though his work is more traditionally associated with vocational education than with correctional education, Pestalozzi is remembered as a pivotal figure in European education history. His influence was general, extending far beyond the places where he worked. His ideas about education appealed to a cluster of important leaders who were eager to improve education in all settings. For example, Froebel, the founder of the first kindergarten, was a student and devotee of Pestalozzi.

Morf, as reported by Monroe in 1912, was one of Pestalozzi's most capable disciples, summarized the instructional method of Father Pestalozzi. The components included:

1. Emphasis on observation or sense perception ("intuition").

2. Language always being rooted in observation of an object.

3. Judgment or criticism being inappropriate when students are learning.

4. Teaching "should begin with the simplest elements and proceed gradually according to the development of the child...in psychologically connected order."

5. Enough time should be directed to the lesson to allow mastery.

6. Teaching is not an exercise in dogmatism, but in development.

7. Teachers must respect students.

8. "The chief end of elementary teaching is not to impart knowledge and talent to the learner, but to develop and increase the powers of his intelligence."

9. Knowledge and power are related; skill results from learning information.

10. Love should regulate the relation between teacher and student, "especially as to discipline."

11. The higher aims of education should regulate instruction. (p. 318).

These findings and sentiments, which seem revolutionary to most modern persons, were even more salient against the backdrop of European education at the time. In short, the approach that dominated education before the work of Comenius, Rousseau, and Pestalozzi was driven by what is known as the child depravity theory. It holds that students are naturally evil, and that the teachers' role is to beat the devil out of them through a focus on discipline, decorum, and rote memorization. By contrast, Pestalozzi's brand of naturalistic education, consistent with the 11 principles summarized by Morf, was driven by human developmental needs. Stated alternatively, Pestalozzi was at the root of modern educational aspirations and practice.

Most books on the history of education will therefore attend to Pestalozzi's great contributions. Readers should know that, whatever the context in which his work is presented, he was a correctional educator in the same school of thought as the others which have been introduced in this narrative.

Summary and Conclusion

McMillan and Schumacher (2001, p. 545) summarized the aspirations that shaped local public schools: liberty, equality, and efficiency—an obvious play on the motto of the French Revolution (liberty, equality, fraternity). But the factors that shaped correctional schools were overcrowding, institutionalization, and reform. The relationship between these two sets of influences describes many of the differences between education "outside" and "inside."

North American correctional education began about the same time as the French Revolution. Institutionalization is the antithesis of liberty—the victory of authority over reason. It results in better inmates and assimilated institutional staff, not better citizens. Social interactions should be based on access to equal opportunities, but this aspiration can rarely be pursued when safety and security in an overcrowded, confined setting is the primary concern.

Reform movements often have a deep, sometimes spiritual dimension. They speak to the essence of the social condition. Education can adapt to any human setting (correctional educators prove that every day), but the forces that drive correctional education diverge substantially from those that drive local schools. Correctional education is more intense, and the issues of human interaction are more visible in confinement. The stakes seem higher "inside," more likely to be interpreted from a life and death perspective.

The influence of institutionalization is easily traced during the 1787-1875 period. Prisons were based on a noble ideal that went bad. Nearly unconstrained discretionary authority resulted in a culture of coercion and manipulation that affected staff as well as inmates. The Pennsylvania system, based on pristine intentions, went bad. It turned robust men and women into solitaires who were unable to function when released. The Auburn system, based on behavioral modification goals, went bad. It reaffirmed coercion and introduced a vast array of manipulative procedures, ultimately designed to be efficient in making profits for the state.

The systems outlined in this chapter developed as a result of overcrowded conditions. Outcasts and criminals from the congested London metropolis populated America, crowded the hulks, populated the Australian continent, and established the preconditions for Reformatory Prison Discipline. In America, the first population centers acted as engines for the new institutional systems. They resulted in the Philadelphia/Pennsylvania system of prison discipline, and then in New York/Auburn system, and later Elmira. The press of urban industrialization led to prison overcrowding, and had a profound influence on the early systems.

However, once each system reached a critical mass, there were opportunities for important reforms. Even managers of the corrections industry are incapable of controlling everything. Prisons themselves were initiated as a great reform. John Howard and Elizabeth Fry set the pace of early prison reform, showing how prisons and prisoners could be corrected. Alexander Maconochie, Sir Walter Crofton, and as we shall see, Zebulon Brockway devoted their careers to improving the world through prison reform and correctional education. Unfortunately, their reforms merely interrupted routine brutality, which followed the reforms they ushered in and resulted in "the hidden heritage" of prison reform and correctional education.

Reform is the key element in this history, the key to system-wide balance. The possibility of reform—for both incarcerates and institutional systems—infuses correctional education with meaning. Institutionalization and overcrowding do not pull at the heartstrings like liberty and equality, but reform is central to modern Western aspirations. The experience of correctional educators can be much more trying than that of our local public school counterparts. However, it can also be more rewarding for individuals and for society as a whole.

With regard to overt physical conditions, the systems introduced in this chapter—Pennsylvania, Auburn, Reformatory Prison Discipline—were progressively better settings for correctional education. Teachers in the Pennsylvania system were rarely able to transcend the constraints of solitary cell study. By allowing congregation, and as a public relations gimmick, Auburn system managers enhanced opportunities for classroom learning and teaching. Reformatory Prison Discipline further enhanced these opportunities, and intrinsically encouraged inmates to improve themselves through education.

With regard to motivation and rationale, the systems had very different goals. The Pennsylvania system was designed to make criminals think right, the Auburn system was designed to make them act right, and Reformatory Prison Discipline encouraged criminals to change their attitudes.

The most salient contributions of the period were made by specific personalities who represented the needs of their communities and addressed the issues with credibility. John Howard opened the public mind to the possibility of prison reform. John Henry Pestalozzi demonstrated how institutional reform and education could be woven together to produce transformative results. Elizabeth Fry showed how influential one person could be in establishing access to literacy. She also shed a light on the plight of women prisoners.

Maconochie implemented programs which demonstrated that institutional systems need not be brutal—they could actually be reformative. Walter Crofton proved that Maconochie's plan could be applied outside Australia, and he expanded on Maconochie's applications. Later Brockway would refine those same applications, and adjust them for an American setting, with special help from Matthew Davenport Hill and Mary Carpenter.

Each of these heroes gained the credibility and authority to reform their system through professional networking. They built formal alliances and informal liaisons, disseminated information to interested audiences, facilitated meaningful experiments to extend knowledge, and worked to replicate proven methods in new environments. Professional networking was the difference between Sarah Martin (who was successful in one gaol) and Elizabeth Fry (who was successful throughout Europe). Networking resulted in Jared Curtis' innovative funding scheme—from the Massachusetts Prison Discipline Society while he worked in New York State—and in his system of bringing in outside seminary students as voluntary teachers. Professional networking was one of the secrets to success of all the great correctional education heroes.

However, each was also helped by professional community associations that nurtured prison reform and correctional education. Early Pennsylvania efforts were facilitated by the Philadelphia Society for the Alleviation of the Miseries of Public Prisons, which sponsored William Rogers' first foray into correctional education. The Boston Prison Discipline Society, and its offshoot the Massachusetts Prison Discipline Society, were crucibles of information and resources for improving institutional education. Their ideological dedication and perseverance sustained early American correctional educators. The New York Prison Association pursued parallel work during the Pilsbury epoch, and set the pace for changes that eventually replaced the Auburn system with Reformatory Prison Discipline in the United States. Correctional educators need and deserve support—from the community, their agencies, and from each other. Professional networking is a tool to develop or obtain that support. In subsequent chapters, the changing associations will be introduced, the associations which carried on the work of these early exemplars.

All these factors—overcrowding, institutionalization, and reform; physical conditions, motivation and rationale, personal influence, heroes, and nurturing associations—can be summarized under two headings. Correctional education has been a result of both systemic structures and individual personalities.

Structure and personality are always present, and rarely in balance. Sometimes the influence of structure predominates; at other times personality sets the pace. This pattern will unfold with greater clarity as this narrative proceeds, but its presence was discernable even at the birth of correctional education. For example, Maconochie, Crofton, and others were willing and able to oppose institutionalization, even in an authoritarian milieu characterized by overcrowding. The positive spirit of their constructive defiance of brutal systems will be evidenced in the subsequent pages.

The 1876-1900 Period

Introduction

The three major elements introduced in the 1789-1875 period remained operational in the 1876-1900 period: overcrowding, institutionalization, and reform. However, they interacted in new and different ways. The historical record of correctional education during 1876-1900 is characterized by a remarkable combination of two of those elements, institutionalization and reform.

Maconochie's Reformatory Prison Discipline bounded from nation to nation, but was managed distinctively in each setting. It took many years for Pilsbury officials to gain legislative permission to implement Reformatory Prison Discipline; then it was implemented by staff who were already institutionalized to the Auburn system. It took more years to reorganize the new system for implementation by existing staff. During the start up and implementation periods, new forms of repressive institutional systems were also developed. New and robust prison reform and correctional education patterns emerged, simultaneously. This was a complicated story, but we wove together the most salient elements in the pages that follow.

Zebulon Brockway and the Elmira Experiment

The layouts of facilities always reveal the founder's, and the management's, program aspirations. At Elmira, the founder and first superintendent (a 26 year tenure) was Zebulon Brockway. The Elmira Reformatory physical plant was monumental. Superintendent Brockway built several school buildings. It was designed to house young first offenders. In its heyday, Elmira had 42 vocational trades, a comprehensive array of academic courses, and other related programs. Elmira was the most serious experiment of the American corrections programming to date, and education was at the heart of its design.

To staff Elmira's schools Brockway hired college professors, school principals, and attorneys as civilian teachers. The size and quality of the professional faculty was unprecedented, for Elmira began when the Sabbath school model was still the reigning paradigm in correctional education. Nevertheless, most Elmira teachers were inmates. They attended periodic inservice training sessions on education, and served under the civilian education faculty.

Brockway organized the institution according to what we now call the principle of social education hegemony, consistent with Maconochie's design in the South Pacific and Crofton's in Ireland. Social education was the priority; all institutional programs were bent toward social education—toward the socialization of offenders. Officers no longer served simply as turnkeys. They assigned marks, and that function encouraged Reformatory officers to act more like teachers than they had under the Auburn system. There was even a woman teacher from Elmira College.

Brockway organized Elmira's industries under vocational education. This diverged starkly from the modern pattern in which vocational education is organized, either officially or unofficially, under prison industries. The modern pattern emphasizes profits, but Brockway's structure was free to emphasize student learning, particularly after 1888 when the Yates Law prohibited selling prison-made products on the open market.

Brockway used this organizational structure to emphasize the educational aspects of the institution. Elmira's architecture, along with its staffing pattern and organizational structure, showed that education was its primary goal; education had hegemony over all other functions of the institution. Reformatories in the United States during this period, all modeled after Elmira, were prisons that were designed in some ways to be transformed into schools.

One of the special challenges of education and institutions during this period, especially in New York State, was to Americanize large populations of immigrants from other countries. Italian, Irish, and Eastern European immigrants were especially numerous during the 1876-1900 period.

Another challenge experienced at Elmira was to identify an appropriate correctional education methodology. Brockway began his career with a very religious orientation. By the time he was at Elmira, however, he had adjusted that view. Instead, he chose to emphasize science. He called it "penological science," and predicted that it held forth the promise to reform any criminal.

For his time Brockway supported academic freedom for both faculty and students. This is a concept that is not discussed frequently in modern correctional education, at least not in the U.S., except occasionally at the postsecondary level. Instead, non-controversial skills are pursued in most modern classes (punctuation, how to divide fractions, learning a trade, and so forth). The emphasis on academic freedom at Elmira may be one of the most salient points of contrast between correctional education then and now. Although Brockway still controlled the curriculum, discussion was encouraged. Topics for teaching and learning were often selected because they were controversial—about truth, the human condition, history, science, religion, politics, and so forth. These were openly discussed, without constraints.

At Elmira there was an initial period of professional identification with local public school education. However, the staff soon noted that local school methodologies did not meet the identified needs of their specific target population. Brockway encouraged the faculty to identify professionally as adult educators, even though there was little available information about how to teach adults outside the college community. The Lyceum was a popular form of adult education at the time, especially in the Northeastern U.S.; Brockway incorporated its cultural education emphasis into the Elmira academic program. These approaches—emphases on education, qualified staff, academic freedom, and adult education—contributed to the unique organizational climate of the Elmira school. The program was an intense and systematic experiment, a quest, to discover how to implement correctional education with minimal reliance on the former Sabbath school model.

Vocational classes included tailoring, woodworking, machine work, blacksmithing, sign painting, printing, furniture caning, carpentry, and others. Vocational shops were constructed like factories and mills. The Elmira architecture, with its stately college-like academic facilities and austere factory-like vocational shops, made a statement about just how transformative correctional education might be in the lives of confined students.

Brockway established a Sunday morning cultural program, each week on a different topic, presented during the time that had previously been applied to formal religious services. This was very popular among students, and it helped maintain good inside/outside community relations. Cultural programs helped Brockway bring in the best speakers and performers: artists, writers, scientists, musicians, and so forth. Brockway himself rarely missed a session. The focus was on what was happening in the world at large. Correctional education was now moving toward secularization in earnest.

The Elmira ethics class was housed in the school auditorium that Brockway had constructed. The ethics teacher took great pride in the pursuit of truth that was allowed in his class, and throughout the entire institution. He bragged that he did not care if detractors called him a communist or a zealot. He only wanted the students to develop the habit of pursuing truth in his class. Brockway was consistently supportive of the correctional education faculty.

There were some problems at the Elmira school. For example, Brockway decided that only inmates who had taken the English Literature class would be released, regardless of how much time they had spent at the institution. Almost overnight, enrollment in English Literature jumped from about 60 to about 500. However, Brockway did not have a collection of English literature books for the students to study until about a year later, when a wealthy Englishman bequeathed his library collection to the Reformatory.

Elmira received frequent visitors, mostly scholars and politicians, from many nations: Germany, Spain, England, and others. In 1895, an Englishman named Ruggles-Brise visited. He studied the Elmira model and implemented it in his own country. This is how the Borstal (open prison) system began in England. Alexander Winter, another Englishman, visited Elmira in 1897 and wrote a glowing book about it which helped to disseminate relevant information to interested staffs. Before the turn of the century then, Maconochie's Reformatory Prison Discipline had been disseminated from the South Pacific, to Ireland, to America, and to England. From there, it would be adopted in the Nordic countries. This became a worldwide reform movement.

The first inmate newspaper was started at Elmira in 1883. It was called *The Summary*, a title that described its purpose. Newspapers were contraband at Elmira and at many other institutions during the 19th century. The purpose of *The Summary* was to present concise synopses of current events stories for inmates. The Summary Press also printed the annual *Elmira Reformatory Hand Book*, and a number of important public relations materials. Soon after the appearance of *The Summary*, the *Annex* was published—an inmate newspaper written on a lower reading level, so all inmates could access information on current events. Although several other institutions in the U.S. began inmate newspapers shortly after the Elmira success, it was only after World War I that they became a general trend in correctional education.

Brockway embarked on a series of experiments to provide education for disabled learners. The manual training class was part of what we would now call the special education department at Elmira. Manual training was becoming popular in public schools at the time, but it had a different focus at the Reformatory. Academic, vocational, and social education were integrated for all inmate students, including learners with disabilities.

Several times a year there were new special education experiments. At the end of each experiment the successful components were added to the ongoing program, and the unsuccessful components were discarded. Physicians and attorneys managed these special education experiments, but Brockway always took the planning initiative. Despite the initial impetus for these experiments being a solution to management problems with this population, a great deal was learned from them. The success of each experiment was rolled into the next program.

Elements of the program for learners with disabilities included early morning instruction, prescribed diets and calisthenics, multi-modal learning—including kinesthetic activities (such as drawing in sand, making clay letters, and working with copper sheets), prescribed clothes (properly-fitted, according to a physician's prescription), and so forth. The categories of disabilities had different labels from the ones we apply today. Special education programs were available for the "incredibly stupid" in one content area (learning disabled), "awkwards" (who had fine or gross motor problems), "incorrigibles" (emotionally disturbed), "kindergartners" (cognitively delayed), "weaklings," "dullards," and so forth.

The indeterminate sentence law that Brockway had drafted to establish the Elmira Reformatory required maintenance of individualized records for all prisoners. Upon entrance to the prison, every body part of each inmate was measured and recorded for identification purposes, as fingerprints were not yet in use. For the special experiments with "incorrigible" or "imbecile" groups, measurements were taken each month, with results recorded, so Brockway could monitor who lost weight and who gained. He had the physician adjust individual diets, adding fresh vegetables and exercises to keep students trim, heavier foods and exercises to build them up.

The Elmira gymnasium was huge. Physical education had been available since ancient times but its first modern, individualized applications were first implemented in the gym that Brockway built. Elmira even had a large bath, with massage spaces and Turkish bath. Pictures of the baths do not appear very fashionable by today's standards, but they were constructed of marble, and had hot and cold running water. It was very luxurious for the late 19th century. The John Howard Association of London (a prison reform group) condemned Brockway for the expense. They called Elmira a "palace prison." He tried not to let criticism interfere with his effort to define the parameters of a successful correctional education program.

Brockway had the bathroom constructed because he became convinced from his special education experiments that a warm, early morning bath would help students learn. He even hired experts to implement a Swedish massage program. Dr. Hamilton Wey, the Elmira Reformatory physician, believed that a warm morning bath and massage would promote learning for some slow learners. The record of program success suggests he might have been correct. Wey implemented a series of experiments with men who were identified as dullards, underweight, slow, or incorrigible. The men would have hot and cold plunge baths, followed by massage and exercise, several times a week. Through the Elmira special education program, Wey and Brockway demonstrated that even low achievers could learn.

Legal Problems of the Elmira Vocational Education Program

For several years a raging debate was pursued in the New York State legislature about the appropriate role of prison industries. At that time, prison products could legally compete on the open market with products manufactured in the free community. This was an unfair policy. Convict labor could be compared to slave labor; outside entrepreneurs and workers could not compete in the marketplace against cheap products manufactured in prisons. It is the same today with manufactures from prison industries abroad, or from nations where workers are paid absolutely minimal wages.

This was a struggle with long historical roots. In 1801, Pennsylvania cobblers had protested the appearance in markets of boots made at the Walnut Street Jail. That battle was solved by requiring that the words "Made at the State Penitentiary" be burned into every boot made with convict labor. However, labels were only a solution to the immediate problem—this issue would not abate. By the 1880s, the controversy was very intense in New York which had more prisoners than any other state.

Indeed, this struggle was only put on hold until the Great Depression of the 1930s, when Federal legislation mandated the "state use system." According to that system, prison industries could only produce materials for use by the state government that manufactured them, within that state's own boundaries. Union leader Samuel Gompers devoted a great deal of effort to advocacy for the state use system during the 1920s. Events culminated with two major pieces of Federal legislation, the Hawes-Cooper Act (1929), and the Ashurst-Summers Act (1935). Nevertheless, this is still a controversial subject. Most modern observers have preconceived notions and emphasize particular aspects of the issue, frequently without access to the historical record. In this heated 1801-1935 continuum of events, New York State's Yates Law was an important juncture.

The 1888 Yates Law forbade all prison industry production. This was an especially difficult challenge for Elmira, because Brockway had organized the entire institutional program according to the principle of social education hegemony. All Elmira industries were managed as components of the vocational education program. The effect of the Yates Law at the Reformatory was that daily vocational education activities were eliminated with the stroke of a pen. Brockway knew that the worst thing would be to have inmates idle during the period they had formerly been in vocational education. Idle inmates frequently become involved in escape plots and inmate-to-inmate violence.

The answer was "military education"—drill practice on the marching field. Brockway conceived this plan on the eve of Yates Law implementation, and the next day he began the practice of having students march up and down in the yard for hours at a time. Then he formulated a rationale that extolled the virtues of military discipline. Like Maconochie, Brockway had started a small musical band early in his tenure at the Reformatory. Overnight, it grew into a big marching band.

The new procedure was explained by the need to combat the dangers of idle time and help men acquire discipline and respect for authority. Eventually, Brockway applied his new special education techniques to this enterprise, with "awkward squads" composed of new men and men with gross motor problems. They wore identifiable, funny-looking hats and uniforms that seemed to emphasize their awkwardness. The physical education department, which had previously served only "abnormals," also expanded to engage the entire population in calisthenics. This story is part of Brockway's autobiography, *Fifty Years of Prison Service*. It is also reported in the Elmira annual *Hand Books*. The men in the military education program used fake wooden rifles that were prescribed by a physician for weight and height. Uniforms were also prescribed (tight or loose), according to each man's identified needs. Brockway's response to the Yates Law was the first example of what we now call boot camp. Despite all the good intentions that were directed toward its implementation, these responses to the new Law contributed to the institutionalization of Reformatory Prison Discipline.

After about two years, the Yates Law was repealed but the new expanded school schedule was maintained and the elements of military education and physical education for the general population remained operational. Despite the idealism of its leadership, its original rationale, and the exemplary spirit of experimentation that had been introduced to keep it on course, the program had become institutionalized.

This ends our brief introduction to Brockway and the Elmira education program. The next pages discuss parallel trends during the 1876 to 1900 period.

Further Institutionalization of Reformatory Prison Discipline

Prisons in the Southern United States did not develop during the early years of the country, as slavery provided a free work force. There were some prisons for whites, but nothing approaching the numbers in the Northeast. After slavery was eliminated, this market was closed. The reconstructed Southern states established prison farms to contain large numbers of former slaves. Many states still have road gangs, or systems of small, movable institutions that were constructed to provide inexpensive convict labor for road maintenance.

The prison farms and chain gangs were brutal. Men assigned to the road quota worked hard under the gun all day and slept in cramped wagons or shacks, often chained to their beds with leg irons. There was not much opportunity, or inclination, for school. The prison farms and chain gangs represent some of the worst episodes in the history of America's corrections industry.

Unfortunately, there was a good fit between the hierarchical relationships that existed in these programs and the relationships sought by Auburn system prison managers. Although the Auburn system had been developed much earlier, aspects remained in many places. Many of the myths and practices that developed in those facilities were accepted at other facilities around the country (they became institutionalized). In fact, those myths have become a basis of modern prison culture.

In most cultures a dichotomy exists between the "head" and the "hand," between those who do manual labor and those who do intellectual or administrative labor. That dichotomy was evident in the college-like academic facilities at Elmira, and the factory-like vocational education shops. One effect of the dichotomy is to make academic skills available to some groups of people, and vocational skills to others.

In the late 19th century African American community, the dialogue between Booker T. Washington and W.E.B. DuBois focused on this issue. Should African American people struggle to learn the manual ("hand" oriented) trades—to earn livings without threatening White people? Or should African American people be encouraged to learn any profession that is available and interesting (even those with a "head," or literary orientation)? The former view was frequently expressed by Washington, and the latter by DuBois. This dialogue is meaningful to modern correctional educators, who see its results every day.

Modern vocational education in local community schools, especially the trade and industrial education which has been so integrated into the correctional milieu, emerged at about the same time as correctional education. Its strengths and weaknesses became part of the fabric of correctional education. Even today, institutional employees are keen to explain how "some people learn better with their hands and others learn better with their minds." This sentiment usually reveals more about racist attitudes than about good educational theory.

Once the hand/mind dichotomy became institutionalized, education became an activity to be pursued, or provided, only when it could produce concrete benefits—only when it would lead directly to increased occupational opportunities. In some institutions there was great reluctance to provide educational opportunities until just prior to release. What was the point of preparing inmates for life in the outside community if they were not likely to be released for another 20 years?

The only appropriate answer, of course, would have been that education is a self-help strategy for all people, regardless of their immediate situation. The only appropriate standard by which institutional schools should ever be evaluated is, "Would I want my child to be educated in a school like that?"

However, narrow and provincial attitudes that would limit human capability became the standard fare of corrections. These attitudes were sometimes expressed by correctional educators themselves. The vast universe of vocational education was reduced almost entirely to trade and industrial education, with an emphasis on the skills needed by a docile workforce. Later, the entire constellation of adult education, with its repertoire of womb to tomb cultural learning and self-actualization, would likewise be reduced to adult basic education "inside." The entire horizon of educational aspirations became reduced almost inevitably to the Three Rs and marketable skills. These attitudes are clues to the extent of how institutionalized correctional education became, at least in the United States.

Anti-education employees frequently found support in prisons. Harsh staff perspectives, forged in coercive Auburn system facilities, were carried over to modern corrections. Technically, the Auburn and prison farm systems no longer dominate the corrections industry. Striped uniforms, the lockstep, road gangs, and real prison factories and farms have waned. However, the spirit of those former systems was transplanted into the fertile soil of modern institutions—including among many education staff. What could be more obstructionist than educators who adopt brutal, anti-education views? Yet that is precisely what institutionalization, the mindless focus on traditional practice, produced—despite the best intentions and heroic contributions of men like Maconochie, Crofton, and Brockway. There are several specific reasons why this problem scarred their remarkable records.

Prior to the professionalization/specialization trends of modern corrections, very few staff were required to operate an institution. Those trends first emerged at the 1870 Cincinnati Congress—with its focus on Reformatory Prison Discipline and its lofty Declaration of Principles—but they did not gather strength for decades. Typically, the entire staff of a large institution consisted of a dozen men or less. Small staffs, the ever present us vs. them logic that dominates relations between staff and inmates, and close hierarchical relations contributed to the institutionalization of Reformatory Prison Discipline by staff trained to implement Auburn institutions and prison farms/chain gangs. A final element was the growth of scientific knowledge, fostered by 19th century racist, sexist, and class-oriented bias.

Early "Scientific" Applications in Penology

Cesare Lombroso was the criminology scientist par excellence. He espoused views similar to what we now call the classical school of criminology. Lombroso was disgusted that judges dispensed various sentences to people who had committed the same crime. He advocated that the punishment should fit the crime (rather than fitting the criminal). Lombroso believed that criminals were responsible for crime, and that uniform sentences should be applied for similar crimes. He actually did indicate that women were more likely to be born criminals than men, a reversal from earlier perspectives about women.

This orientation diverged from the reformatory prison discipline ideal, because it was based on the idea that criminals would not or could not change. During the early 20th century, the classical school was contrasted with the emergent sociological school which attributed responsibility for crime to the social environment. A diluted form of this logic resurfaced during the 1970s and '80s, associated with the sociopath and criminal personality theories.

Lombroso contributed to the "born criminal" argument, the reasonable conclusion of associating criminality with anatomy. The logical next step was that, since some people were born criminals, it was in society's interest to confine them before they had an opportunity to commit crime. Lombroso himself was not as responsible for the application of this logic as some of the scientists of the age who applied his theories.

Around this time, the Eugenics movement became very popular. Advances in science led to increased understanding of genetics. Eugenics, or the "science of human betterment," suggested that certain deficits were genetic in nature, and a cure for them would be to prevent defectives from producing children. This led to the largely unsuccessful practice of marriage laws, and the very successful (in terms of numbers) sterilization of defectives and prisoners.

Thomas Mott Osborne, a great prison reformer and correctional educator of the early 20th century, found that there was no convincing evidence of any "born criminal type." In his speeches and books, Osborne steadfastly ridiculed scientists who equated the shape of a person's nose or brow with a predisposition to commit crime.

However, Osborne did maintain that there was a prison type—that confinement interrupted maturation and changed a person's life. There was a "prison type" of person. In this, Osborne paralleled Dickens' earlier comment, that he could spot a man recently released from Philadelphia's solitary prison, even in a room full of men who had never been incarcerated.

The late 19th century was the heyday of phrenology and the Bertillon method of identifying people. Phrenology asserted that criminal behavior could be predicted through the study of certain body parts, especially the shape of the skull and face. The Bertillon method predated fingerprints for identification purposes. It consisted of intricate measurements of all major body parts, since no two people have exactly the same proportions.

The fingerprint procedure succeeded the Bertillon method of identification. Fingerprints were suggested by Mark Twain, in a story he wrote called *Puddin'head Wilson* (1894). The protagonist was a detective who tricked a criminal and solved a crime by getting fingerprints left on a drinking glass. This story was published about the time of a terrible mistake in which two African American convicts with the same name, and approximately the same size, age, and weight, were tragically confused. This incident showed how the Bertillon method was flawed. Despite all the intricate measurements, it was not conclusive in the identification of specific people.

Another scientific application in penology focused on the "mystery fluid," electricity. History notes that the first electrocution took place at Auburn Prison in 1890, with an axe murderer named William Kemmler as the first recipient.

The electric chair was a result of a business war between the companies that eventually became General Electric and Westinghouse. Future revenues from the U.S. electricity market were at stake. The purpose of the electric chair was actually educational—to demonstrate that since alternating current (AC, the kind of current we have in our houses) could kill people, it could not be used safely.

Nikola Tesla advocated AC, and built dynamos and equipment capable of providing AC in residences and factories around the country. Westinghouse adopted Tesla's concept. Thomas Edison, on the other hand, advocated direct current (DC, the kind of current produced by batteries). The company that became General Electric supported Edison's plan. These were the contentious factions of this money-making war.

Edison (General Electric) purchased Tesla (Westinghouse) AC generating equipment, laundered through a South American country so Edison's reliance on the enemy (Tesla) in this war would be difficult to trace. He began electrocuting small animals at his West Orange, New Jersey laboratory: mostly cats and chickens, then dogs. Soon he demonstrated that he could kill cows and horses with AC, as well. Then a lobbying effort was mounted to make the electric chair a legal substitute for hanging. Amid this fanfare, the public was supposed to get the message—AC kills people, so it is logical to support DC for the growing, potentially lucrative electricity market. Edison successfully implemented the electrocution; the death, though nearly botched, was messy enough to send a strong message to the public. However, DC was so impractical for residential wiring that Edison's scheme never won much support. To use DC on a wide scale, special generators would have to be constructed on almost every street corner. Eventually, our residences and industries were all wired for AC. Tesla lost the battle, but his system won the war—the electrocuted ax murderer just lost.

This ends our brief review of the 1875 to 1900 period, which corresponds with Brockway's tenure as Elmira superintendent. Brockway left the Reformatory amid controversy about the prison's programs. The dispute was between some newly installed members of the Elmira Board of Managers and an Elmira vocational instructor.

Brockway was elected mayor of the town of Elmira almost immediately after his retirement, and went on to attend the international prison discipline conference and pursue a career of writing on prison reform and correctional education. Zebulon Brockway died in 1920. The next chapter will begin with the year after Brockway quit his full time job as superintendent of Elmira Reformatory, 1901.

Summary and Conclusion

The remarkably close interaction between the forces of reform and those of institutionalizetion was the salient attribute of correctional education during the 1876-1900 period. Maconochie's Reformatory Prison Discipline was an exemplary system. It represented the hopes of prison reformers all around the world because it held promise of reversing the psychological damage associated with both the Pennsylvania and Auburn systems which predated it. Reformatory Prison Discipline was adopted in the United States at Elmira, after successful implementation in Ireland; from Elmira it was disseminated to England. However, it suffered from institutionalization at each step along the way. In the U.S., Reformatory Prison Discipline was implemented by staff and managers who were accustomed to the harsh Auburn system. At approximately the same time, new repressive Jim Crow penal systems were emerging in the former Confederate States, and the field of penology found new rationales for the segregation and brutalization of inmates.

The 1901 to 1929 Period

Introduction

This period began after Zebulon Brockway retired from the Elmira superintendency. It ended when the first draft of Austin MacCormick's nationwide survey report appeared.

Several exciting processes would unfold during the first decades of the 20th century. They were built upon the work of the previous, prison reform-oriented period—the epoch of Maconochie (Australia), Crofton (Ireland), and Brockway (United States). The heroes of the 1901-1929 period were eager for prison reform through emphases on citizenship and democracy—the principle of community organization. The idea of lifelong segregation caught on in some places, because if someone was a born criminal, it was best to keep him incarcerated. Although still dominant, the forces of institutionalization were sometimes outclassed and defeated, or at least neutralized for a few years. New traditions were forged in correctional education by a new breed of heroes.

Library Work

This is the story of how a librarian from a remote Midwestern county focused her energy to help provide library services for convicts all over the country. Miriam E. Carey, the librarian in Iowa's Burlington County, was upset because convicts did not have access to InterLibrary Loan services. We do not know exactly what prompted her concern. Perhaps a relative or neighbor was incarcerated. When Carey learned that there was no "inside" access to InterLibrary Loan, she organized petitions to the Iowa State Board of Control, the agency that managed the State Library. After years of coordinated effort, the Board of Control adjusted its policy. InterLibrary Loan services were extended to the penitentiary and other institutions. In 1907 Carey was assigned to head up a new Institutional Department of the Iowa State Library.

In 1908 Minnesota pirated Carey by offering her greater administrative authority to help accomplish the same objective in that neighboring state. Like Moses Pilsbury in prison management, Carey established a dynasty of professional prison librarians that eventually acquired nationwide influence in prison libraries and prison education. Perry Jones was trained by Miriam Carey and succeeded her; Mildred Methven was trained by Perry Jones and succeeded her.

Perry Jones made contact with the Carnegie Corporation. Andrew Carnegie, who had established a huge steelmaking empire, wanted to direct some of his profits back into local communities. He focused on libraries because they were needed and appreciated, and could help improve lives. Today, many towns have libraries that Carnegie constructed or enlarged. The Carnegie group also supported prison libraries in the U.S. and England, with funding and political support. Perry Jones provided an important service by liaising between the prison library community and Carnegie decision-makers.

One result of this great flow of events was that every state library established a department to coordinate aspects of institutional library services. Another result was Austin MacCormick's survey of prison libraries and prison education—which changed correctional education for all time and will be the subject of further discussion in this chapter. A third result was that during this period the American Correctional Association and the American Library Association established a joint Institutional Libraries Committee which has remained influential since Mildred Methven's time. Through concerted efforts that began with county librarian Miriam E. Carey in Iowa, the world was improved a little bit.

Reform Schools for Juveniles, and their Relation to Prisons

Other aspects of 20th century life needed improvement, as well as libraries. For example, unruly youth and their involvement in urban crime was a highly visible problem of the 1901-1929 period. Truant officers were charged with responsibility for rounding up juvenile delinquents, to make sure they would stop being bothersome to neighborhood businesses and residents. Juvenile delinquents were treated as adults in court. Eventually this practice was recognized as inappropriate because children were seen as not fully accountable for their actions. In 1899 the first juvenile court was established in Illinois. This procedure decriminalized the processing of child offenders. A principle of the new system was that youth should receive treatment instead of punishment—a change which often led to longer time spent in custody. Without the court procedures, juveniles might stay much longer in the institution than they would if convicted for the same offence, and often did.

William George was a New York City businessman who was concerned about juvenile delinquency. In 1895 he started a summer camp in rural Long Island which gradually became a year-round juvenile institution. George believed there was something healthful about rural life, that it could be an antidote for the problems so evident in city life.

George was also patriotic. He believed that, since the U.S. Constitution was the best plan to organize the nation, it might also be the best plan for organizing an institution. Therefore, he managed his institution like a republic, according to the principles of the U.S. Constitution, and called it the Junior Republic. That is also the title of his 1911 book on the subject, a handbook about how to replicate his successful program. Everyone else called his institution the George Junior Republic, but he modestly referred to it as simply the Junior Republic. Today Junior Republics are still operational in several states.

Early in this adventure, George embraced a simple rule: "nothing for nothing." Juveniles who did not work received limited food and no new clothes. This has been interpreted as an extension of the democratic principle into the economic sphere, as well as in the governmental.

The republican form of management extended to every aspect of the institution except the school, because State law required that licensed teachers had to be in charge of educational activities. Every other program—even the facility budget and personnel matters—were handled by the students, while George assumed a back seat role.

The students elected their own institutional congressmen, senators, and a president who appointed a supreme court to oversee disciplinary procedures. They established a chocolate biscuit factory to help raise funds for institutional maintenance. The whole experiment was a grand success. George's book is very readable, full of pictures and touching and interesting stories about the special challenges the wards overcame.

One of the most interesting challenges came when the girls at the Republic refused to continue cooking, sewing, and paying taxes unless they could become citizens and the right to vote extended to them. They initiated a job action and lobbied the institution's elected officials. A vote was taken among the boy citizens, and the Junior Republic Constitution was amended to extend the franchise to Republic girls. This change occurred before the 1920 passage of the 19th amendment to the U.S. Constitution, which resulted in the same reform on a nationwide scale. Thomas Mott Osborne elegantly summarized the George Junior Republic program:

> ...the Junior Republic is but one brilliant example of...the Democracy which is a political expression of the Golden Rule.... I hope I may live to see the day when in every school and college in the land alongside of the standard of Scholarship may be raised the standard of Citizenship....Gladstone said: 'It is liberty alone that fits men for liberty.' (Osborne, in George, 1911, pp. ix-xii).

Osborne was an upstate New York politician, a Harvard graduate, and a millionaire industrialist. He was mayor of the town of Auburn, and editor of the newspaper there.

Lucretia Mott, Osborne's great grandmother, had been a Quaker abolitionist before the Civil War. Osborne lived in a mansion that had been constructed as a station on the underground railroad. It had been used to smuggle escaped slaves to Canada. The house had secret passageways and compartments. Osborne grew up in an environment that resonated with reform.

As a child Osborne had been taken to visit Auburn Prison, in his home town, but most of his adult life was devoted to priorities other than prisons.

Like John F. Kennedy decades later, Osborne's mother had told him that he would grow up to be president—and Osborne believed her. Most of his political career was a struggle to organize the reform wing of the Democratic Party, and to defeat the corrupt influence of Tammany Hall.

In 1908 Osborne's bid for the national Democratic presidential nomination suffered a setback at the hands of the old free-silver candidate who would later be associated with the anti-evolution attorney in the Scopes "Monkey" Trial, William Jennings Bryan. The record suggests that if Osborne had not taken an anti-imperialist stand against the American military annexation of Hawaii, he might have become president. Nonetheless, he did take that stand, and as a result he did not receive his Party's nomination for the office. Osborne's whole political career was aborted, much as Maconochie's had been when he was left unemployed in Hobartown.

Osborne served on William George's Junior Republic Board for about 15 years. He was appointed by the elected juvenile president to a justice assignment in the Junior Republic Supreme Court. Osborne was affectionately called Uncle Tom by the juveniles. They loved him because he cared about them as individuals, and were always excited when his big car arrived on the grounds. Osborne was one of George's most influential supporters. From George, Osborne had learned that democratic procedures could be implemented in juvenile institutions.

In 1895 Osborne had visited the living authority on correctional education, Zebulon Brockway, at Elmira. He wanted to see how a model prison should be managed. Their meeting was rather uneventful; Brockway and Osborne did not really like each other. The import of Osborne's pilgrimage to Brockway was that he recognized the old man's authority in prison reform and correctional education, and that he was intensely concerned about those important issues. Osborne and Brockway were concerned about the human adventure, and recognized that there was a special drama being played out "inside," and in the relationship between "inside" and "outside."

One day in 1912, confined to his house with an illness, Osborne read *My Life in Prison* (1912), about the San Quentin experiences of Donald Lowry. Gradually, a personal plan for a new career in prison reform emerged in Osborne's mind. Would it be possible to apply George's democratic principles in adult prisons? If yes, would that be a uniquely American way to correct the glaring prison problem—precisely the problem that the Auburn, Pennsylvania, and the by then institutionalized Reformatory Prison Disciplinary systems had left unsolved despite all their original motivations?

Osborne visited his friend the New York governor in 1913 and got himself appointed chair of a new Blue Ribbon Prison Reform Committee. With the governor's letter of appointment in his pocket, Osborne went to Auburn Prison to chat with the warden.

Inmate Tom Brown

The result was that Osborne was voluntarily incarcerated for about a week, as a forger. He became Inmate Tom Brown in order to "learn about the prison business" from the inside. Officially incognito but nevertheless known by inmates as a celebrity, Osborne worked in the knit shop making socks, lived in a cell, ate the same food as the other inmates, and was even locked in solitary confinement for a few days. This story is told in one of Osborne's great books, *Within Prison Walls* (1924a).

This experiment left the Auburn Prison convict population fervently enthusiastic about the possibility of reform and improvement. Within a few weeks they organized into a Mutual Welfare League (originally known as the Golden Rule Society). With the warden's permission, the League managed every aspect of Auburn Prison. The inmates took over the prison through duly elected representatives. This was an experiment; William George's juvenile institution management model would be adopted, expanded, refined, and consolidated.

The initial meeting that founded the League was a scene of high intensity and excitement. Osborne addressed the convened general inmate population in the chapel. He asked the officers to leave him alone with the men, and they complied with his request. This was a totally unprecedented expression of trust in the men, who responded by meeting the challenge. They lived up to Osborne's highest expectations, and the League was established by unanimous vote. It was a wonderful victory for everyone, and a new lease on life for many who would otherwise have been crushed by the Auburn system.

The experiment was a great success. League constituencies were established on the industrial democracy model. Electoral districts were not based on housing units, as would have been expected if the League was structured exactly according to the U.S. Constitution. Instead, each prison industry shop had representatives on the League Committee that managed the institution. Every aspect of the prison came under League control—housing, industries, even discipline. An inmate court was established, parallel to the Supreme Court at the George Junior Republic to which Osborne had been appointed. This George/Osborne innovation represented an improvement over Maconochie's program, because it went a step further than the Norfolk Island open hearings procedure.

The League established a satellite unit outside the walls—a prototypic halfway house—and named it after their hero, Tom Brown. Inmates assigned there said their only problem was that women kept coming around to visit them. However, the inmates were so committed to the League system that they shunned this attention and dedicated themselves exclusively to the program's success.

In this new regime the Auburn guards actually had very little to do. They just watched as the democratic process developed. A recreation program was started, and the whole Auburn milieu became healthier. Outside visitors came weekly, and were escorted by inmates so they could observe and monitor League progress. Some of the visitors were high-profile luminaries and officials, friends of the program's greatest advocate, Thomas Mott Osborne. They invariably became friends of the convicts, as well.

Industrial production at Auburn skyrocketed; escapes, assaults, rapes, and contraband were almost eliminated. Osborne's program was compelling to the inmates; it commanded their interest and support. Osborne brought positive peer pressure to bear in matters great and small. He accomplished this by always working indirectly, without being preachy, and letting the men make their own decisions—even when they decided foolishly. No one wanted to be responsible for undermining the League and bringing back the Old System (the hated Auburn system of prison discipline). The effect of this experiment was that convicts role modeled good, community-oriented behavior for other convicts, and provided positive support for positive behavior. The League motto was, "Do Good, Make Good."

The obstructionist corrections managers in the Statewide central office were furious about all this. Osborne was giving away their much-coveted control, and establishing a successful precedent that would undermine their own discretionary authority. The Statewide Corrections group in Albany plotted and schemed. Eventually, they decided that the way to get rid of Osborne was to have him appointed to a responsible, highly visible position—a "set up" that would be designed to fail. They offered Osborne the warden's job at Sing Sing.

Sing Sing Warden

In preparation, the Albany group transferred bullies, snitches, and stoolpidgeons—anybody who could be manipulated—to Sing Sing. They were desperate convict leaders, who resented Osborne's program because League success meant a reduction of their unofficial, personal authority. The difference between the convict bullies and the Albany good-old-boys, at least in their attitudes toward the League innovation, was marginal. The capital gang was nervous about protecting its official authority, and the convict gang was nervous about protecting its unofficial authority.

True to his democratic principles, Osborne sought advice from the elected Auburn League representatives about whether he should accept the Sing Sing warden's job. The advantage of accepting that appointment would be that the proven League model could be replicated at another location. The model was reasonably secure at Auburn: there had been many good articles in the newspapers, the warden and most of the staff were genuinely committed to the League's success, and the democratic process had already established a record of unparalleled success. The disadvantage was that the Sing Sing assignment was clearly a devious "set up." Osborne would be personally vulnerable there—and he was the outward symbol of the whole League program. Sing Sing would be a terrible risk and a great struggle, but the chances of revamping the Old System throughout the New York State prison community seemed almost within grasp. The League encouraged Osborne to take the new assignment, so he did.

At Sing Sing warden Thomas Mott Osborne witnessed a repeat performance of the Auburn triumph. He helped the inmates establish another Mutual Welfare League, according to the same parameters as the one at Auburn. Again, it was a grand success; again it was front page news, with a regular stream of visitors and observers; again the good-old-boys felt profoundly threatened.

This time the dynamics of the drama were experienced more intensely, because the stakes were higher. Sing Sing's Mutual Welfare League represented further expansion and refinement of the Auburn structure. The Sing Sing League established a program to share work with officers, so officers could enjoy more weekends at home with their families. League members (convicts) worked as officers when needed, on the walls armed with rifles, to prevent escapes. When someone did escape, Osborne armed a group convicts and sent them out to retrieve the culprit. After all, if an inmate escaped it would be reported as a League failure and the whole program might be put in jeopardy. Some of the stories about how positive peer pressure was used to convince escapees to return were amazing. One good book on the League was by Frank Tannenbaum, *Osborne of Sing Sing*. It was published in 1933, and has an introduction by President Franklin Delano Roosevelt.

At one point, Osborne sent a large group of prisoners out into the community to attend a history lecture in which they had expressed interest. He personally borrowed about a dozen cars from his friends for the event, since no official Prison vehicles could be appropriately used for that purpose. Osborne allowed the convicts to drive the cars, without an officer escort. While they attended the lecture, a terrible blizzard began. On the way back to the Prison, the driver of the last car in the caravan lost his way. The whole Sing Sing community was in alarm, because all but one carload had returned. No one wanted an escape. However, the solitary car returned early the next morning, and everyone was relieved. The inmates had been driving all night, lost in the snow.

Over 90% of the Sing Sing population was enrolled in school during this period. New school buildings were constructed to accommodate the tremendous program expansion. The League named its education program the Mutual Welfare Academy, and delivered on its promise that a qualified teacher would be provided for any branch of study that an inmate wanted to pursue.

As time went on the Albany group worked to coordinate its attack on Osborne and the League. Sing Sing is located in Westchester County, New York, and that was the scene for the struggle against Osborne and the Mutual Welfare League.

Legal Battle with the Good Old Boys

In Maconochie's case the community of free Australian settlers had complained to the Home Office about his penal reforms. Osborne's case was not quite so simple. He had developed good community relations, and enjoyed the active support of a large group of community leaders. The real opposition to the League was centered in the Albany corrections office. Nevertheless, some community members believed Osborne had single-handedly diverted the traditional Sing Sing emphasis on punishment. The Albany office capitalized on this scattered resentment, and planned that the case would appear to be initiated by the Westchester County prosecutor. Battle lines were drawn.

The prosecutor accused Osborne of permitting homosexual activity at Sing Sing, and of not bringing cases of sodomy to the criminal courts. This charge was unprecedented. Sodomy had been a fact of life in prisons, but no other warden had ever been brought up on charges of not referring relevant cases to the criminal courts. It was widely accepted that wardens had responsibility over this type of case, and could handle it through internal disciplinary action. The concept had never been previously challenged. Osborne's actual crime, of course, was that he had delegated disciplinary authority to the Mutual Welfare League courts; it had nothing to do with the issue on which he was tried.

The prosecution secretly promised transfers to convicts who memorized false charges for testimony. The prosecutor promised that previous inmate leaders would be reinstated to their old positions of informal power once Osborne was removed from office and the League disbanded.

The Auburn and Sing Sing branches of the Mutual Welfare League communicated with each other regularly. They established an "outside" branch of the League to help coordinate public relations and fund-raising for legal support. That branch later became the National Society of Penal Information; it is known today as The Osborne Association, Inc. The outside branch held big rallies. For example, they had Osborne speak at Carnegie Hall, colleges and universities, and other locations, and kept up a constant stream of literature about prison reform and correctional education in the popular press. He was a great speaker and writer, very informed on the issues, very persuasive, always fair. Osborne spoke and wrote with authority, because he knew the subject. He was the unquestioned authority in the field. The legal defense was extremely costly, but the coordinated inside/outside fund-raising support activities paid almost the entire cost.

This story was consistently front-page news. The prosecution's case was not convincing. It was riddled with trumped up charges and contradictory testimony. Eventually, the charges were overturned, and Osborne was fully acquitted.

Victory, and Expansion of the League Model

Osborne was so closely identified with the League that his defense had been a defense of the League concept. Almost everyone was extremely pleased, except the Albany group and the few treacherous inmates who testified against Osborne.

The assistant Sing Sing warden had maintained League procedures during Osborne's absence, so he could prioritize the legal defense. When the charges were dropped, the League staged a grand homecoming celebration for their triumphant warden. Inmates actually rolled out a great red carpet for him at Sing Sing. They prepared a huge banner with the greeting, "Our Friend, Our Pal—Inmate Tom Brown." Former graduates of the Auburn and Sing Sing League programs were proud to be associated with Osborne and their colleagues who were still inside. They flocked to the homecoming ceremony in great numbers. Speaker after speaker reviewed the successes that the League had attained, and the profound meaning of those accomplishments. Inmates got the discarded "Auburn-style" striped uniforms out of the Sing Sing basement, and did a skit that mocked what they called "the Old System," before democracy came to the Prison. There was an immense crowd at the victory celebration, and their joy was heartfelt. Everyone was glad of the victory. However, Osborne was tired from the fight, it had weakened him.

Osborne's Navy Career

Franklin Delano Roosevelt, Osborne's great friend and upstate New York Democratic colleague, saw through the fanfare of the highly publicized return to Sing Sing. Roosevelt realized that the legal defense had been very taxing on Osborne. Roosevelt was undersecretary of the Navy at the time, following in the footsteps of his cousin Theodore. With American entry into World War I, Roosevelt saw his chance to give Osborne another assignment, one in which he would not have to defend himself against official resentment of his humanitarian approach to convicts.

Like William George before him, Osborne was a patriotic American. However, his age prohibited enlistment in the military. Instead, Roosevelt had him appointed warden (commodore) of the U.S. Naval Prison in Portsmouth, New Hampshire.

And Osborne did it again. Within a few weeks, a Mutual Welfare League was in operation at Portsmouth Naval Prison.

He reported a funny story about the Naval Prison in one of his Yale lectures, the series that became the text of his book *Society and Prisons* (1975/1916). The following passage describes an event at Portsmouth when an officer needed counseling.

After the Mutual Welfare League had been in operation at the Portsmouth Naval Prison for over two years, my Executive Officer left for a few month's sea duty; and in his place Lieutenant C., an officer of long experience in the service, reported for duty at the prison. During the first day he looked about; found upwards of 2000 prisoners, most of them living in barracks outside the prison—with no bolts or bars and no wall about the grounds; saw a number of prisoners go down to their work in the Navy Yard, accompanied by a few marine guards; saw the rest going about their duties at the prison without any guards at all; saw the working parties return and the guards march away to the marine barracks; saw the third-class prisoners entirely under the charge of their fellow prisoners of the first-class; saw, in short, an unguarded prison run by the prisoners. At the end of his first day, Lieutenant C. came into my office looking pale and disturbed. 'Commander Osborne,' he broke out, 'I can't stay here.' I looked up from my desk. 'What's the trouble?' 'I can't stay here,' he repeated; 'I'm scared to death. Why don't these men all run away? I would.' Now, don't get excited about it,' said I; 'sit down.' He did so; and as he dropped into a chair, he fairly groaned. 'I don't understand it.' 'Well,' said I, 'Lieutenant, I will tell you something. Please don't give me away; for this is a secret. <u>I don't understand it either</u>. I've been trying to understand it for six years—ever since I got into this prison game; and I haven't succeeded yet. However, don't let it worry you; it is not necessary that either of us should understand it. We know, as a fact, that they do not run away; and experience proves that we can proceed with perfect security upon that fact. Now you may explain it any way you like, but I may as well tell you that I shan't care a snap of my fingers for your theory; and my theories are of no particular value or interest to you or any one else. Not only that; I have not a single theory or idea about this prison game that I am not ready to alter or throw away the moment it bumps up against a fact. We are learning new facts every day here; because we are dealing with real, live human beings—the most interesting things in the world.' The Lieutenant seemed somewhat comforted; but as he glanced out of the window, the troubled look came again into his face. 'But you haven't any wall here, or even a fence!' 'No,' said I; 'we haven't; and I'll tell you why. When those barracks were built, they had a beautiful plan all mapped out with a high and heavy steel fence which could be electrified and protected by barbed wire; and this was to go on the water-side as well as the land-side and spoil that fine view, that does us all good to look at. I went to the Commandant and said: 'Admiral, for heaven's sake don't let them put up that monstrosity. If we have a fence that is hard to climb, of course my boys will all want to climb it. Put up a light wire fence that any fool can get over, and I'll see that they don't get over it.' So they put up that chicken-wire stuff that you see. Do you know what I have said several times at mass-meetings to these fellows here?' I continued. 'I have told them: "Of course you know and I know that it's dead easy to get away from this place. I should be ashamed of any one of you who couldn't escape from here.' But I always added: 'I should be ashamed of any one of you who did.' Do you know what is the number of escapes we have had here? Eight, out of over six thousand prisoners! And only think how easy it is! And we have had none at all since our last marine guards went over-seas and the prisoner police have been on the job. More than that, Lieutenant—' But all that is another story. If more people had seen the Mutual Welfare League in operation at the Naval Prison during the years 1917-21... (Osborne, 1924b, pp. 44-49; emphases in original).

The Portsmouth program was reviewed with great commendation from all quarters. It rehabilitated men who had been taken out of active service, so they could be reassigned to combat positions in the War. The League was a patriotic program. After the war was won, Osborne returned to a more comfortable schedule of writing and speaking for prison reform and correctional education, and doing some visitations and consulting work. In *Society and Prisons* Osborne wrote

...the thing works...the thing works....In Auburn prison for more than two years, in Sing Sing prison for more than a year, the new system has been in operation and the thing works....it works. (Osborne, 1975/1916, pp. 222-233; emphases in original).

His refusal to develop a theory about why it worked represents a point of departure between Osborne and several other prison reformers who tried to categorize democratic prison reform procedures, to make them clinical or scientific so they could be replicated cookie-cutter fashion.

The League was a brief shining star in correctional education history, parallel to Maconochie's brief tenure at Norfolk Island. The whole League process was so tied up with Osborne's personality that his death in 1926 was sorely felt. Nevertheless, Osborne proved that democracy can work, even in prisons.

The Mutual Welfare League program amounted to an interruption of the coercive/manipulative regime that had dominated Auburn, Sing Sing, and the Portsmouth Naval Prison before Osborne's arrival. The whole phenomenon is usually discussed in terms of its effect at Sing Sing, because that place had the worst reputation before the League, and it returned to its previous condition a few years after Osborne died. Coercion and manipulation dominated Sing Sing again when the League was eliminated by State officials after a 1929 riot.

The League had transformed Sing Sing into what Osborne called "a large class in social ethics" (1975/1916, p. 229). The prison yard became a place where everyone discussed the rights and wrongs of interpersonal, ethical, community issues. The Mutual Welfare Academy looked and felt like a school; it certainly emphasized student learning. But the real result of the principle of community organization was that it got the men thinking and talking about personal and social development—how to live together in peace, with dignity. A prison had become a school.

This aspect of Sing Sing deteriorated after the demise of the League. Later, for several years, administrators even changed the institution's name, a futile attempt to improve its terrible image. It was renamed Ossining, after the town in which the Prison is located. The old coercive style returned quickly. In terms of correctional education, student learning needs were no longer prioritized after 1929. Osborne's contribution is a major theme of this text, but our current task requires that we move on to related, important trends of the 1901-1929 period.

Progressive Trends in Reformatories for Women

During this period the movement for women's reformatories gathered strength. There was an historic sequence of institutional operations for incarcerated women. In the very early period, before classification, men and women were thrown into the same confined settings. This resulted in the "riotous debauchery" of the English gaol scene.

Zebulon Brockway's Detroit House of Shelter, where Emma Hall worked as matron and social education teacher, was the first annex built for women only. This innovation set the pace for female annexes to mens' prisons, within institutional walls or compounds. Gradually, these annexes became separate buildings, still within the compound. That was better, but women still did all the domestic work for the prisons—cooking, washing, sewing, ironing, and so forth. The annexes were frequently managed by male officers, a situation which created many problems.

The Prison Association of New York was established in 1845. The women members left in 1854 to start their own organization, the Women's Prison Association of New York (WPANY). This group advocated separate facilities for women prisoners, with women staff, administrations, and programs tailored to women's needs. Soon, women got a foothold in charity administrations, and a long struggle began. In 1861 the WPANY received a financial contribution from a group of New York City reformers.

The Sing Sing Women's Prison was within the institutional compound, and was known as Mount Pleasant. It had a monumental facade and some grand architecture. Typically, women's annexes and prisons were beautiful. Some even had fine carpets, oil paintings, antique furniture, and sweeping staircases in the sections of the institutions that were accessible to visitors. Nevertheless, they were places of confinement.

The whole progression toward separate prisons for women was driven by several trends. First, gender was—and still is—the best predictor of incarceration. In most systems, even intentionally, only 5% to 10% of the incarcerated population is female.

Second, cultural perceptions shaped female incarceration in ways that were more obvious than in male institutions. Historically, women had been put "up on the pedestal," and they were looked to as the nurturing, supportive, pillars of family and community. That was just another way of saying that "fallen women" had come a long way down. According to this view, women criminals must be worse than men criminals, because they originally occupied such an exalted position. Programs were slow to start, as there was no perceived need for them with such a population.

Third, these cultural perceptions suggested that the problem of fallen women was that their men had not been taking care of them. Their "cure" must therefore be greater emphasis on domestic skills, to enhance success in traditional, male-dominated relationships after release. The preferred solution was not personal transformation, but a match with a better man than before. Additionally, there was a real question whether any treatment could be successful at all with women who had fallen so far from their natural tendencies. Conventional perception suggested that if any treatment could be successful it would be preparation for a traditional relationship with a good man. These views reflected the cultural biases of the period.

The WPANY advocacy effort was an attempt to break out of this cycle of blaming the victim. WPANY was unsuccessful at first. However, during the Civil War female criminality rose to unprecedented heights. This problem was attributed to the observation that most men were away fighting and could not take care of their families so some females made up the difference with income from their criminal careers. The female criminal population grew rapidly, and became more visible. This same phenomenon occurred during the Irish Potato Famine of the 1850s. Records there indicate that 50% of the prison population was female in Ireland during that time.

Periodically, incarcerated women became pregnant by their jailers. In some of the worst cases, the staff who impregnated them beat or murdered the pregnant women, apparently to hide the evidence. These episodes were the stuff of newspaper sensationalism. Increased attention was focused on women's issues during the period, a result of the early feminist women's suffrage movement. Kate Richard O'Hare's 1923 book *In Prison* gave a good account of the conditions faced by women confined in male prisons.

During the 1885 to 1915 period, women's reformatories were built in several states. Framingham (Massachusetts), Bedford Hills (New York), and Albion (New York) were the most famous. Clara Barton, the famous Civil War nurse, served as a reform warden for a few years at Framingham. The Massachusetts governor was a retired Civil War general who stridently proclaimed that if Barton did not take the job, he would offer it to a man. This was too much for the emergent women's groups to accommodate. Barton took the job for a while. She did famously, and was a strong supporter of correctional education.

Eliza Mosher became superintendent of Framingham, the Massachusetts reformatory for women. Formerly employed as the institutional physician, she was a good, humanitarian warden. Mosher established a progressive program, capable of helping women who were interested in becoming relatively independent upon release. One of the things for which she is most remembered was her steadfast refusal to segregate Framingham according to race. Eliza Mosher did not cooperate with Jim Crow segregation. The good-old-boys in the capital eventually removed her from office and rolled back the innovative dimensions of the program. They required a traditional emphasis on women's work and prayer, in a racially segregated setting.

This was the period of the emerging sociological school of criminology, which succeeded the classical school that had dominated during the previous period. A school of thought is a worldview shared by a group of colleagues who network, study, and explain the paradigm and their program aspirations to interested audiences. The sociological school of criminology was centered at the University of Chicago.

According to the old classical school, criminals were entirely responsible for their own behavior. This view emphasized the "nature" part of the nature/nurture continuum that describes the causes of crime. According to the new sociological school, however, environmental or social factors fostered criminal behavior. This view emphasized the "nurture" part of the continuum.

Networking was intense among advocates of the new women's reformatories. They were all connected through the activities of the sociological school—conferences, program planning, funds solicitation, speaking engagements, correspondence, mutual studies and writing projects, and so forth. By about 1912 this group of leaders and researchers proved that, instead of being the cure-all for female crime, domestic work in traditional relationships was actually a cause of female crime. The best modern books on the subject of women's reformatories are by Estelle Freedman, *Their Sisters' Keepers* (1981), and Nicole Hahn Rafter, *Partial Justice* (1985).

Katherine Bement Davis was the warden at New York State's Bedford Hills, the showcase female reformatory. Davis was a very important member of the sociological school, and she mobilized a number of research projects at Bedford Hills. This was a period of great antagonism between people who wanted to maintain traditional roles among the genders, and those who articulated the shortcomings of those roles and worked for equality. In a way these issues became encapsulated and reflected in the women's reformatory movement.

For example, the Italian criminologist Cesare Lombroso (of the classical school) reported that criminals were born with certain physiological traits. That view supported the popular phrenological approach, which predicted criminality through analysis of anatomy, especially the shape of the head and face. This popular view held that scientists could examine a person to identify whether that person was a "born criminal." If a person was destined to a life of crime, there would be little value in correctional education. Lombroso had decided "scientifically" that all females were born criminals. The sociological school worked hard against this perspective, and women were in the forefront of the struggle.

In 1907 there was a white slave scare in the Northeastern United States, fueled by newspaper sensationalism. Reports of innocent young girls being sold into prostitution came out, and Americans were very angry about it. Almost immediately, people became concerned about the welfare of prostitutes. This concern shaped the education programs of the emerging women's reformatories, and facilitated the implementation of the programs sociologists advocated. It also prompted John Rockefeller, the robber baron of Standard Oil fame, to direct funds to sociological school research. He set up the Bureau of Social Hygiene adjacent to Bedford Hills. Jean Weidensall was the main sociological school researcher at Bedford Hills.

Sociological school data suggested that female crime was triggered by poor environmental conditions: alcoholism in the family, poverty and poor housing, proximity to crime, prejudice based on ethnic background, prostitution in the neighborhood, and so forth. This information helped counter traditional values, which tended to blame the victims of poor environments. It also helped counter Lombroso's orientation that women were inherently criminal.

The Bureau of Social Hygiene had a eugenics agenda. Eugenics, or the "science of human betterment," was an approach which suggested that, since mental defectiveness and criminality tended to run in families, sterilization was the answer. Over the years, many Bedford Hills women were sterilized at the Bureau of Social Hygiene, as they were in institutions all over the country. Often the officer on the cellblock determined who needed sterilizating.

One of the emphases of the new reformatories for women was that females should have access to vocational training in alternative careers, to lessen traditional dependency on men. One example was secretarial work, though today this hardly seems an alternative career for women. During the early years of the 20th century, however, typing and stenography were bastions of male privilege. At Bedford Hills Reformatory for Women, typing was a nontraditional or alternative career for women. It was foolish and unrealistic to wait for men to come along to take care of them after release. Instead, the reformatory staffs embarked on education programs that would help a released woman earn her own living, in jobs that were selected for compatibility and good pay.

This view was not accepted in all the women's reformatories, and it was not maintained during and after World War I. Indeed, tradition suggested that confined women should be taught to pray, sew, cook, and so forth, so that they could be hired out as domestic workers to middle class families after release. These procedures resembled the indentured servitude procedures of colonial America, or the outright slavery of the Australian penal colonies. It is interesting to note that these women, who were considered so dangerous they required incarceration, upon release are brought into peoples' homes to live and work. Instead, the alternative career orientation was an important part of women's reformatory education programs during much of the 1901-1929 period. Concern about nontraditional training for women prisoners continues to this day, and has had limited success.

Davis was a leader in this important movement. She supported democratic procedures, and announced to the world that the purpose of Bedford Hills was to equip the women for life in a democratic community—even though this was not what they would encounter upon release. Even though the 19th amendment to the Constitution providing for women's suffrage had not yet been passed, women needed to learn about and participate in democracy, at least while inside.

Several of the leaders of the women's reformatory movement were in touch with Thomas Mott Osborne, and aspects of their programs were parallel to those of the Mutual Welfare League. At Bedford Hills and the other sites where women were involved in outside work, physical education and vocational education went far beyond domestic training. The women at these institutions were truly being prepared for life in democratic communities, just as Davis had announced.

When America entered World War I, the sympathy and concern that had been demonstrated toward prostitutes turned into its opposite. Instead of being concerned about the welfare, protection, and education of prostitutes, Americans became disgusted by them. People were concerned, instead, that their sons in the military might contract venereal disease from prostitutes. The transformation of women's reformatories, which had begun to emerge around 1885, had its heyday only from 1907 to 1917. The weight of traditional programming in the institutionalized setting was so heavy and pervasive that the innovations of 1907-1917 were swept away in a tide of sentiment that reinstated domestic training and the emphasis on traditional roles for women. This reactionary movement replaced the gains of the earlier period.

Correctional Education for Southern Blacks

Reaction is the hallmark of institutionalized systems. In 1921, however, the Board of Directors of the Virginia State Penitentiary embarked on some specific reforms. Thomas Mott Osborne visited Richmond at the request of the Board, and he encouraged them to implement a comprehensive reform program. For the first time, classes for "coloreds" were organized. The students were treated as defective delinquents, but the effort was important. The term defective delinquent had been applied to those young offenders who demonstrated deficiencies in academic or social areas. Being classified as such might occur simply by being placed in a facility for defectives.

Throughout the South separate Jim Crow institutional systems for African Americans and Whites had been established. Typically, there were four systems, separated by race and gender: one for White boys, another for African American boys; one for White girls, and another for African American girls. This was expensive and took a long time to develop. In Virginia, the State established institutions for White boys and for White girls. However, it was often up to the African American community to mobilize private funds for the two institutions for African American boys and African American girls. The alternative was that African American children in conflict with the law would be sentenced to adult jails or prisons.

Janie Porter Barrett was president of the Virginia Federation of Colored Women's Clubs. She helped mobilize funds for African American juvenile institutions. The institution for African American girls was named after Barrett. It was organized according to a cottage plan, with progressive housing. In other words, parts of Maconochie's plan were implemented. Federation Honor Cottage at the Janie Porter Barrett School for Girls was named in honor of the Federation of Colored Women's Clubs.

Most of the separate institutions for African American girls adopted the traditional programming model, with an emphasis on domestic training. Almost invariably, after the African American community of a state would invest funds to establish their own institutions, the state would move in and take them over. Today most of these institutions are managed just like any other state funded facilities.

Anton Makarenko and Soviet Education

The last major episode we will consider of the 1901 to 1929 period is from the Soviet Union. Anton Makarenko, a correctional educator, is known alternatively as "the hero of Soviet education" or "the John Dewey of the Soviet Union."

Makarenko lived in the Ukraine and was educated at a normal school (a school for teachers). The period of World War I, the Bolshevik Revolution, and the resultant Civil War, had left the area in ruins. The military front had shifted back and forth across the Ukraine time and again, and the results were devastating. This situation was similar to the one that Pestalozzi had encountered in Switzerland after the Napoleonic Wars. The Ukraine commissar of education called on Makarenko to establish a colony (institution) for juvenile delinquents.

The wars had left millions of hardened juvenile delinquents throughout the Soviet Union. Many of them had never known normal, civilized life. They lived from hand to mouth, and were involved in all sorts of criminal activity. Some were aged 13 or 14 and had not yet acquired the ability to speak because they were so alienated from normal society.

In 1922 the commissar of education gave Makarenko control over a recently nationalized estate to use as an institution. Makarenko started reading books on education, and gradually took in a population of delinquents who needed shelter and a place to grow up. He named the institution Gorky Colony after his friend and mentor author Maxim Gorky, and tried to care for the children with the ridiculously meager provisions offered by the State.

The children raised their own food, despite the fact that no one at Gorky Colony knew anything about farming. They eventually established blacksmith and carpentry shops, and bartered these services for food among the villagers and peasants. They stole sometimes, too—farm produce, bread, fish, etc. Sometimes they went hungry. Makarenko attracted a small circle of dedicated teachers who staffed the institution. He used the Komosol program, which was like a combination of a young Communist Party and the Boy Scouts, to help develop self confidence, teamwork, and discipline in the population. Leaders in the Communist Party often shared a background of Komosol membership.

Makarenko's main literary contributions were *The Road to Life* (1973), a trilogy about social education at the co-ed Gorky Colony, and *A Book for Parents* (1954). Maxim Gorky edited Makarenko's books. *The Road to Life* was read as great literature in the Soviet Union until about 1988, when the political climate changed. The books are enchanting. Episodic like a novel, they focus the reader's attention on the meaning of community life in a difficult setting. Makarenko's role in the U.S.S.R. was in many ways parallel to John Dewey's role in the U.S. Local public school staff in the Soviet Union looked to correctional education models as the new Soviet standards of excellence.

This reversal of what many consider the normal relationship between correctional education and local public school education did not come quickly. The books on education that Makarenko read after the commissar assigned him as juvenile institution administrator were mostly written from a Deweyan perspective. Makarenko rejected this approach, saying that the individual philosophy Dewey recommended was inappropriate for education in the Soviet Union. Instead of exalting the individual, he said, Soviets should help to prepare youngsters for life in a collective society.

Makarenko got in trouble with the Bolshevik education establishment by rejecting the Deweyan perspective. He was totally alienated from the early Soviet education community, and frequently in trouble with various education commissars. Nevertheless, he maintained his original position in the argument, and in the end he certainly won out. Soviet education was eventually rooted in Anton Makarenko's philosophy, not in John Dewey's. Nevertheless, Dewey and Makarenko became friends. Dewey visited him in the 1930s, and they made a movie together, also called *The Road to Life*.

Makarenko's alienation from the Soviet education community during the early years of the Gorky Colony was so intense that it inhibited his ability to feed the children. Soviet bureaucrats were unwilling to allocate scarce resources to someone who was in rebellion against their established system. At the end of this period, the only real advocate Makarenko had was "the Butcher" Felix Djerzhinski, who had helped establish the Cheka secret police (an offshoot of which developed into the KGB espionage organization). Djerzhinski was one of the few leaders Lenin trusted. In addition to his state police assignment, Djerzhinski was given responsibility to establish a government nurturing capability to bring all the wild orphans into the Soviet lifestyle—hence his support for Makarenko.

In the midst of a terrible famine, the Cheka built palace prisons for Makarenko's juveniles, complete with parquet floors, vaulted ceilings, and stained glass windows. When Stalin came to power, Makarenko's procedures received official public approval and Makarenko became an overwhelmingly popular celebrity. This relationship was solidified in a speech Stalin delivered in 1935. All sorts of people looked to this correctional educator for advice in all sorts of situations. He was one of the most influential Soviets of his time.

Readers should not assume that this association with the KGB and Stalin means his work was negative or brutal. Makarenko was of the same school of thought as Maconochie, Brockway, George, and Osborne—he emphasized personal responsibility and social maturation for offenders as the precondition for successful community life. For a few years, Makarenko corresponded with Thomas Mott Osborne about key elements of the democratic school of thought in prison reform and correctional education.

Stories about life at the Gorky Colony illustrate Makarenko's link to this democratic school of thought. One of the major problems at the Colony was feeding the children and staff. The children were accustomed to thievery, so when they were hungry they went into town and stole food, or raided the peasants' fishing nets or orchards. Makarenko was able, through a series of events, to turn this problem around to such an extent that local peasants voluntarily contributed foodstuffs to the Colony. When a girl became pregnant at the institution and then killed her baby, Makarenko was worried that the authorities would close the institution. As it happened, they did not.

Makarenko was concerned about the anti-Semitic attitude that many children exhibited toward one of the Jewish residents, and he used it as an object lesson. This became one of the biggest personal crises he faced. He was enraged at the prejudice the juveniles displayed, and frustrated that the children were not listening to his message about correcting the situation. At one especially difficult moment, Makarenko lost his temper and punched one of the children. The child did not suffer much more than an assault on his dignity. This punitive behavior was totally opposite to the way Makarenko wanted to act, and he was immediately disgusted with himself for responding violently toward the stubborn child. However, that event marked the turning point in the Colony's history because it began a new level of communication. From the time he lost his temper and punched the student, the children began listening to his advice, and were generally much more cooperative.

Makarenko's social education program grew stronger and stronger. Bonding and mutual support took over; students became productive instead of parasitic; hooliganism was no longer an issue. Law enforcement did not initially emerge intact from all the wars. Makarenko eventually armed the children with real rifles, and sometimes sent them out into the villages that sought their help in breaking up illegal stills and gambling rings. The worst punishment that could be applied for misbehavior was to be released from the institution. Makarenko had developed a democratic institutional community, Soviet style.

From time to time Makarenko was puzzled by great social problems during the early years of the Revolution. His personal response was to become quiet and stay by himself to focus on the problem, sometimes for a month or six weeks. Then he would emerge and announce the potential solution. This was the procedure by which he struggled with the problem of Deweyan philosophy, and the result transformed Soviet education.

Another problem that haunted Makarenko was the Bolshevik attitude toward the family. The Communist Party had taken preliminary steps to attack the nuclear family unit. There were multiple reasons for its actions. For example, allowing women to pursue careers was an achievement in the struggle for equality between the genders; it also unleashed productive forces in the Soviet Union. But another dimension of the initiative was that it attacked traditional family roles. The new divorce law was extremely fair, but it was seen as an assault on the family unit. Also, the Soviet leadership was convinced that the traditional family pattern was a bastion of conservative, paternalistic influence in society, and they were poised for further action to ensure its demise.

According to his habit Makarenko went into seclusion to focus on the problem. When he emerged he announced that the family was an educational collective, and that it advanced the Party's agenda for educating youth. By this time Makarenko was a highly visible personality, and people took what he said very seriously. His attitude helped change the Party's position toward families, while retaining the limited progress that had been made in relations between the genders.

All of Makarenko's work was directed toward the development of what he called "the new Soviet man." Soviet society needed courageous workers capable of thwarting traditional roles, sharing resources, and protecting the Revolution. The development of this type of citizen was the purpose of the Gorky colonies, and it became the purpose of Soviet mainstream education.

Another time Makarenko became concerned about the effects of single child families. He was convinced that "only" children became spoiled and focused on their own individual needs. That focus was antithetical to social aspirations for the new Soviet man. Makarenko went into hiding to consider the issue. When he came out, he wrote *A Guide for Parents*, which set out the reasons for his concern. His advice against single-child households was taken very seriously in the Soviet Union, and later, for a period, in China.

Just before he died Makarenko was concerned about the Soviet response to organized religion. He went into hiding to focus on the problem, but he died before he re-emerged into social life. If Makarenko had lived for just a month longer, it is possible that the decades of Soviet persecution against organized religion might have been averted.

Summary and Conclusion

The emphasis on citizenship that characterized the 1901-1929 period emerged from and refined the previous emphasis on reform. Citizenship, and democracy or participatory management—discussed as "the principle of community organization," flourished under the leadership of George, Osborne, and Makarenko, in the new reformatories for women and African Americans, and in the prison library movement. This was a period of important progress. In turn, these improvements became the basis for the next period in the history of the prison reform/correctional education movement, which spanned the years 1930 to 1941.

The 1930 to 1941 Period

Introduction

The long awaited circulation of Austin MacCormick's draft report, *The Education of Adult Prisoners*, ushered in this period. It ended abruptly with America's entry in World War II.

MacCormick's exemplary contributions, and the field's interpretation of them, dominated these "golden years." The magnitude of MacCormick's accomplishments was comparable to Brockway's; they surpassed them in dissemination. In the 19th century, Brockway had popularized information about the principles of Maconochie, Crofton, and Brockway himself. In the 20th century, MacCormick reiterated many of Brockway's fundamental concepts; in addition, he presented the principles of George, Osborne, and MacCormick himself.

MacCormick was an incredibly big-hearted, gentle, popular, savvy, and successful champion of correctional education. He promoted evolutionary reform by applying concepts from the emerging discipline of adult education. Although many of the principles of adult education were later diluted (institutionalized) in corrections, into what we now call adult basic education, MacCormick himself never took part in that dubious process. Instead, he sought to professionalize correctional education by implementing proven adult education strategies in corrections. His most salient contributions accrued from his work to professionalize correctional education. MacCormick challenged the field to "seek a high aim."

Like the modern period, the 1930s were marked by overcrowding and institutionalization. There was a strong reform agenda, but it was only pursued with caution and diplomacy. The reason for this shift in style was directly related to Osborne's Sing Sing experience. A flamboyant and persuasive organizer, Osborne had won every battle—but after his death the traditionalists rode roughshod over the Mutual Welfare League, and reversed most innovations. The revolutionary aspirations of the 1901-1929 period were therefore muted during the 1930s, and a deliberate appeal was made to conventional-minded institution administrators. Thus recast, the reform agenda gained widespread acceptance. That acceptance was the major theme of the 1930-1941 period.

The Library Connection

The institutional library tradition began in earnest with Miriam E. Carey during the 1901-1929 period, and was carried on by her successors Perry Jones and Mildred Methven. Their solicitation of Carnegie Corporation funds was a turning point that influenced correctional education far beyond the immediate needs of library services. A long chain of unusual events and processes unfolded that would shape correctional education for many decades. That story is summarized in the following paragraphs.

As a graduate student and instructor at Bowdoin College in Maine, Austin MacCormick was preparing to do his masters thesis in 1915. He wanted to study prison reform. MacCormick wrote to the acknowledged master of prison reform, Thomas Mott Osborne. The return letter that he received suggested that the student and the master should repeat Osborne's Auburn experience: they should get dressed up like convicts and study prisons from the inside. Osborne made arrangements with a U.S. Senator from Maine to write an undercover exposé on conditions at the Maine State Prison. The "student and teacher" pair was voluntarily locked up for a week. The pair worked well together. They wrote the report for the Senator, exposing prison brutality.

Meanwhile, the Minnesota Institutional Library group (Jones and Methven were in the leadership during this period) brought Carnegie philanthropists together with leaders from the American Library Association and the Adult Education Association. This coalition group made a call on MacCormick. They were preparing a nationwide survey of prison libraries that would (a) be funded with Carnegie money, (b) take two or three years to complete, and (c) result in recommendations for improving prison libraries. Osborne's able young assistant would represent the Mutual Welfare League as the nationwide study coordinator. The deal was set.

MacCormick and the first Nationwide Study of Prison Education

When FDR had Osborne appointed as warden of the Portsmouth Naval Prison in 1917, MacCormick became deputy warden. Eventually, the person who had started as a graduate student became known as Osborne's right hand, and as his logical successor in the prison reform business. Osborne died in 1926. Convicts honored "our pal, Tom Brown" and mourned in silence.

During 1927-28 MacCormick visited 110 of the 114 prisons in the United States for what was supposed to be the first nationwide study of prison libraries. MacCormick established a study review board to read his draft report, with notables such as Jane Addams, Franklin Delano Roosevelt, criminologist Harry Elmer Barnes, Felix Adler, and two members of Osborne's family. Without consulting the board, however, MacCormick decided to divert the study from its original library purpose, to include prison education in general—including libraries, instead of focusing only on prison libraries.

MacCormick's 1927-28 visits profoundly encouraged the correctional education community to professionalize. Previously, correctional educators had thought of themselves as cut off from others, assigned to dreary prisons without access to information about the education programs in other jurisdictions, or even in other facilities within their own jurisdiction. Some correctional educators actually believed no one else was providing, or had ever provided, educational services in institutions. MacCormick broke through all that by explaining how education was conceived, organized, and delivered at other locations within their state, and in other states. As the survey developed, he circulated galley drafts of his chapters, complete with recommendations about how to use available resources. The effect was overwhelming—it was the beginning of the modern correctional education movement.

However, his visits themselves did not produce much useful information about programs that were ready for replication as models throughout the field. The grand experiments of the previous periods were exactly that, experiments that had not been followed up or adopted. Correctional education was in a shambles.

> Not a single complete and well-rounded educational program, adequately financed and staffed, was encountered in all the prisons in the country. (MacCormick, 1931, p. 38). The educational work of most prisons, in brief, consists of an academic school closely patterned after public schools for juveniles, having a low aim, enrolling students unselectively, inadequately financed, inexpertly supervised and taught, occupying mean quarters and using poor equipment and textual material. (p. 40). [N]o prison in the country has a program of vocational education worthy of the name... (p. 100).

These were terrible problems. MacCormick could disseminate information about specific aspects of programs that had developed records of success. However, he could not point to a good, comprehensive program anywhere in the country. There were no models. Another approach was required if he was going to communicate useful information, capable of influencing field-based practice.

So instead of writing about successful models that were in place, MacCormick started almost from the ground up. He had to establish a compelling model, based on the best available thinking. Of course, he relied heavily on the excellent theory and records that Brockway had left behind. On page xii MacCormick wrote, "In all fields of education, theory is in advance of practice...our practice is always behind our belief."

His report was actually a handbook on how a good prison education program could be organized and implemented. It had chapters on the reasons for correctional education, and on how to do academic education, vocational education, social education, cultural education, institutional libraries, the supervision of instruction, jails education, education in reformatories, and education in women's facilities. Some parts of the book are now out of date, but on the whole it remains more meaningful than almost any other book on correctional education that has been published since that time.

MacCormick's chapters described how good correctional education should be practiced. Much of it was synopses of model adult or vocational education programs outside corrections, summaries of Brockway's principles that could be updated and applied, and outlines of the principles established by George and Osborne. These ideas were often presented without reference to the pioneers of the past. It was, and is, an extremely timely book.

Shortly after Osborne's death, the traditionalist corrections leadership in Albany made life very difficult for anyone who had worked with Osborne or the Mutual Welfare League. MacCormick's book was published by the National Society of Penal Information, which was the new name of the "outside" chapter of the League. The Society was all that remained of that once vital prison reform organization.

The words of the title itself, "The Education of Adult Prisoners," were borrowed from a phrase Brockway used in his 1870 speech at Cincinnati: "The education of adult prisoners must not be neglected" (Brockway, 1969/1912, p. 407). Many of MacCormick's key concepts were gleaned directly from Brockway. Indeed, MacCormick's research was directed precisely to the question that had driven Brockway's quest: What would be the attributes of an exemplary correctional education program?

In other ways, especially in his chapter on social education, MacCormick borrowed from Osborne's work. Demonstrating his courage and integrity in a period when Osborne's associates were being "purged" from State service, MacCormick's book was "Dedicated to Thomas Mott Osborne, of whose epochal work education in its broadest sense was the keystone." His book summarized the theory and practice of good correctional education, in a forthright, readable style.

From the largest perspective, however, MacCormick's work represented the application of proven adult education theory and practice into correctional education. In this sense it is on a scale of Grundtvig's epochal work in the Danish folk school movement, which democratized culture and education throughout Scandinavia and the Low Countries. There are some associated issues that warrant consideration because modern readers might tend to misunderstand.

First, readers should be cautious about often-expressed conventional attitudes toward theory and practice. MacCormick was a great hero of prison reform and correctional education, and he looked to theory as a vanguard element of the correctional education movement. The old dichotomy between theory and practice is illusory at best; at worst it alienates practitioners from useful information. Theory is not inherently bad, and practice is not inherently good. Indeed, our task is to blend them together for the sake of the clarity and effectiveness that facilitates student learning. Praxis is surely good: the application of useful theory in the educational practice at a particular location. A slogan from the environmental movement is applicable for praxis in correctional education, "think globally, act locally."

Second, many modern correctional educators who have not had access to the history of their profession take exception with the term "correctional education." The term "corrections" seems a euphemism for prison, it appears to lack forthrightness, to excuse brutality. For its historical meaning, however, we should explore the term's original context. Thomas Mott Osborne advocated the term "correctional" because it paralleled his humanizing, democratic, New Penology program. "Corrections" meant transformative, as opposed to brutal. MacCormick was at Osborne's side, and he shared stewardship over that program. The change in terminology from prisons or penal, to corrections or correctional, is attributable in part to MacCormick's massive influence throughout the field. MacCormick founded the Correctional Education Association and the *Journal of Correctional Education*, and he applied that term to signify the prison reform/correctional education link. Modern practitioners, often alienated from the literature of their own profession, have forgotten this original intent. The intended meaning of theory/practice and correctional may require a bit of a leap for modern practitioners but the concepts are important aspects of MacCormick's message.

The Education of Adult Prisoners was the culmination of all the correctional education activity that had gone on to that point, and the foundation of all that would follow. It included vast sections on the individualization of instruction, and on group instruction, and suggested that both approaches should be used in the same program. Anyone who wants to know about correctional education should read MacCormick's book (AMS Press reprinted the original edition in 1976).

The Federal Bureau of Prisons

In 1930 president Herbert Hoover responded to a crisis in the Federal prison population. Prohibition and hard times had swelled the ranks of Federal prisoners, and the traditional system of contracting with state prisons to warehouse them on a per diem basis was no longer tenable. There were too many idle prisoners; they needed programs.

Hoover appointed Sanford Bates to be the first director of the new Federal Bureau of Prisons. Bates was smart. Like Osborne before him, he selected Austin MacCormick as his assistant. Then Bates put MacCormick in charge of education. Who would be better? He had recently completed the first nationwide survey of correctional education, and had written the definitive book on that subject. The appointment required that MacCormick move from New York City to Washington, D.C. It also delayed publication of his book until 1931. However, the Mutual Welfare League was no longer the exemplary organization it had been before the reactionary crackdown, and the new Federal job promised vast opportunities to improve prison education. MacCormick was integral to progress, and was respected by key decision-makers and field-based workers alike.

The organization that later became the Correctional Education Association was also established in 1930. At the American Prison Association (APA) conference, Austin MacCormick was appointed chair of the new Standing Committee on Education. This event was another direct result of his book. In 1946 the Standing Committee became an APA affiliate—that was when the title "Correctional Education Association" was born. By founding the Standing Committee, MacCormick formalized the inservice/dissemination work he had started informally in 1927-28 for the Carnegie group, and for the American Library and the Adult Education Associations. Instead of relying on his continuing visits and personal efforts, the Standing Committee would now maintain the work of professionalizing correctional education. The modern professionalization effort was emerging.

Organizational Developments in New York State

Franklin Delano Roosevelt's contacts with Osborne and MacCormick also facilitated expansion of professionalization. The origin of those contacts was introduced in the last chapter. Another of FDR's contributions to correctional education came before he was president, while he was still serving as New York governor.

In 1929 Roosevelt set in motion a new commission, and a series of events that would establish a new kind of administrative structure for correctional education. That structure is now called the correctional education bureau. It was the brainchild of the MacCormick and Roosevelt team.

The bureau was a refinement that departed from the old decentralized structure in which wardens were in charge of every aspect of the institution, including education. It established a statewide cadre of education supervisors in the Corrections Department central office. This made logistical support accessible for teachers, and helped put educators more in charge of educational decisions. The bureau was an organizational improvement that was good for morale. It was the state-of-the-art structure for organizing educational services for confined learners at the time, fostering educator enthusiasm and dedication.

The governor who succeeded Roosevelt in New York was named Lehman. The Commission that FDR had established to plan the bureau was renamed the Lehman Commission. Several events had led up to this point.

Under previous governor Al Smith, Adolph Lewisohn had completed a survey of New York State correctional education in 1920. He found serious inadequacies: no vocational education was in place, inmates were transferred without regard to their studies, low status accrued to the prison schools, no supervisory support of any consequence was available, competition existed for inmates between school and work—with school as a permanent loser, and so forth. Lewisohn wrote the truth about the status of correctional education. No one paid much attention to his report at the time, but the problems could not be ignored.

In 1925 new statutes were introduced for New York State correctional education, parameters for curricula, and staff qualifications. An important step was initiated—correctional education was relocated in State government. Previously located in Corrections, it was now placed under the responsibility of the State Department of Education. While this new strategy was different, it was not better. Most education leaders with statewide authority had only a dim idea of the challenges and opportunities of correctional education. Their professional preparation and overwhelming duties did not permit an emphasis on the new program element. By 1929 the law was changed again and correctional education was placed back under Corrections.

Also in 1929 Sing Sing burned, along with several other prisons in the State. The authorities blamed the Mutual Welfare League for the riots. Historical records suggest the League was not responsible. However, the League was disbanded and inmate membership was forbidden. A statue of Thomas Mott Osborne was taken down and put under wraps in the basement. Employees who mentioned his name put themselves in danger of losing their jobs.

In addition, MacCormick had written an entire chapter of his widely read book on how ineffective the school at Elmira, which Brockway had established and refined, had become. Inmate-teachers were in use, military education had been reduced to a series of sterile procedures without a rationale, terrible old texts were still being used, and in general Brockway's showcase education program had become static and uninspired. Elmira had become a well-publicized embarrassment.

These four events (the Adolph Lewisohn report, legislative changes, riots, and MacCormick's scathing review of Elmira) led to an awareness that something had gone terribly wrong with corrections in New York State. That awareness led to FDR's study commission, which was renamed the Lehman Commission. It was coordinated by Sam Lewisohn, the son of Adolph Lewisohn who had written the critical 1921 correctional education report. The Commission hired Walter Wallack, from Teachers College, Columbia University to overhaul the Elmira school program. Teachers College had been nurtured and influenced by John Dewey (Guelzo, 2005, Lecture 24).

Columbia University faculty had advocated reform of correctional education since 1907, when David Snedden completed his dissertation there on education in juvenile institutions. Snedden's correctional education work had contributed to the vast urban school movement; now he was a Columbia professor. Urban schools of the early 20th century relied heavily on reformatory models, and Snedden's outlook was consistent with the Columbia tradition. Wallack fit right in that tradition, and would eventually contribute to it.

Wallack successfully reorganized the Elmira school. Then he was moved to a new job as director of education in the Albany office—Wallack became the New York State director of correctional education. As such, he was the first statewide director, heading up a new bureau of correctional education. (The Federal Bureau of Prisons had implemented the bureau model a few months before New York State, and MacCormick himself was actually the first correctional education bureau director—but he was not employed by a state.) In summary, the bureau concept was born when Roosevelt was New York governor; it was implemented first in the Federal Bureau of Prisons, under MacCormick; Wallack became the first state director of correctional education.

People all over the country looked to New York State and the Federal Bureau of Prisons as the exemplary correctional education systems. The conditions that MacCormick had reported in his book—that there were no systems with programs worth replicating—was changing. Correctional education was still ripe for improvement, but some important progress was being made.

Patterns that would endure for generations were established during the 1930s. Even today, despite the fact that a better model has been developed, more states have correctional education bureaus than any other organizational structure. The bureau system eventually became institutionalized, like everything else in corrections. In modern times, the bureau model has become to correctional education what the Auburn System was in the last quarter of the 19th century: an outmoded structure that has lived past its usefulness because it got good press from highly visible and credible sources (Roosevelt and MacCormick). Nevertheless, the bureau was innovative in the 1930s, and much more effective than the totally decentralized system it replaced.

One of the first things Wallack did was to consolidate officer training under the auspices of the education bureau. Who would be better qualified to train new officers than teachers? One of the great advantages of this consolidation was that new officers were indoctrinated during their preservice about the advantages of offering education programs for inmates. Wallack eventually did his doctoral dissertation on this topic, called *The Training of Prison Guards* 1937.

However, officer training was just one small part of the improvement program established by the New York correctional education bureau. Wallack established new special education and vocational education programs, made inroads into group counseling, started a handout clearinghouse of teacher-designed instructional materials, and founded a correctional education inservice program with specialized college courses for correctional education teachers. The best book on these New York innovations in correctional education was by Wallack, Kendall, and Briggs, *Education Within Prison Walls* (1939). They selected the title as a play on the title of Osborne's book about his voluntary incarceration at Auburn, *Within Prison Walls* (1924). This was a way to show their appreciation of Osborne's contribution without saying it directly and thereby reaping the wrath of the Albany traditionalists.

In Wallack's office, the authors of the book each played an important role. Glenn Kendall was in charge of academic and social education, and Howard Briggs was in charge of vocational education. During this period, everyone in New York State took for granted that the division of the bureau into academic and vocational units was for administrative purposes only. They all understood that a rigid division between the two would be folly. It was widely believed by this group that the real function of prison education was to help inmates adjust their attitudes, so they could become properly socialized. That was one of the main messages of MacCormick's book, and the stated rationale for the legislation that implemented the New York State correctional education bureau.

Wallack coveted his relationship with MacCormick. Wallack would talk to MacCormick, and then the New York correctional education employees would talk to Wallack. The bureau chief had met the woman who would become his wife at the National Society of Penal Information, the old "outside" branch of the Mutual Welfare League. Wallack eventually left the bureau job to become warden of the new showcase institution, Wallkill Prison, which Eleanor Roosevelt had helped design. Its exterior is still so beautiful that many people think it used to be an old monastery. Later, Wallack moved to Haiti and the Dominican Republic.

Another Norfolk Experiment

Massachusetts began construction of a new prison in the late 1920s. It was named Norfolk, in honor of Maconochie's Australian penal colony program of the 1840s. Howard Gill supervised Norfolk's construction and became its first warden. The prison opened in the mid 1930s.

Gill announced that he would improve on Osborne's Mutual Welfare League program. He was able to establish a relatively participatory prison milieu, but never received the inmate support that had been extended to Osborne. Central office traditionalists quickly managed to eliminate Norfolk's program potential by dumping—transferring inappropriate inmates to the new institution. Gill tried to include officers in the democratic community. He lost a legal battle with State officials and his program was terminated. For decades after the fiasco, Gill was reportedly working on a clinical manual about how to scientifically implement a rehabilitative prison program. As far as we know, this was never finished.

Albert Einstein and Correctional Education

In 1935 the inmates at Illinois' Stateville Prison got fed up with the poor school services there, and they organized their own school. It began as a correspondence school, out of a cell, but eventually became fully accredited by the Cook County School Board. Through the mail, Albert Einstein helped the inmates develop their math curriculum. It was a very successful venture.

MacCormick's Career

MacCormick left the Federal Bureau of Prisons to accept a New York City job in 1934. During his four years with the Federal Bureau, he had gone around the country expanding schools at Federal prisons, hiring principals and assistant principals, starting libraries, and counseling staff about how to build a sound correctional education system. Many of his plans were so advanced that they were still prototypical in the mid-1950s.

MacCormick became the New York City Commissioner of Correction in 1934, under mayor Fiorello LaGuardia. The convicts were basically in charge of the prison when he came into office, and there was a terrible contraband problem. MacCormick cleaned it up, started a fine school program, and earned a reputation as a fair administrator. He was known for his midnight shakedown raids on Welfare Island Penitentiary, to confiscate contraband.

Beginning in 1935 MacCormick became a long-time member of the national Alcoholics Anonymous Board of Managers. He was at the 1935 Akron, Ohio meeting that established the organization, registered as a nonalcoholic participant. He served in several national AA offices during the succeeding decades. MacCormick always maintained a residence in New York City, and he frequently went to the Bowery to buy lunch for alcoholics, just to make sure they ate an occasional healthy meal.

In 1937 MacCormick became the first editor of what later became the *Journal of Correctional Education*. In the first years, before World War II, this journal was simply called *Correctional Education*. A handbook on correctional education was published annually, but the process lasted for only two years, 1939 and 1940. The War interrupted it. The 1939 handbook was *Correctional Education Today*, and the 1940 handbook was *Correctional Administration, an Educational Process*. The handbook tradition was revived in 1989 by Stephen Duguid, of Simon Fraser University, in British Columbia. The old handbooks and new yearbooks remain excellent sources of guidance for correctional educators today. They have been published periodically since.

MacCormick served as president of the American Prison Association, which later became the American Correctional Association (ACA), in 1939. That was the year when most of the ACA conference workshops were about correctional education. Until his death in 1979, MacCormick consistently told the ACA leadership group that he would not attend the national conference unless it was held in a "dry" town. They expressed their respect and support for MacCormick by complying with his wish. It was not until after his death that the ACA annual meetings began to be held in towns that were known for their alcohol and nightlife.

MacCormick left the New York City assignment to serve as warden of Chilocothe Prison in Ohio, which began as a Federal institution. He had helped plan that prison, and admired the programming possibilities. MacCormick served there for four years. Then he coordinated American military prisons in Asia. President Roosevelt awarded him the highest civilian medal of honor for that service. After the War, MacCormick maintained two jobs, one on the east coast and another on the west coast. He taught criminal justice at Berkeley, and directed the Osborne Association in New York (the old National Society of Penal Information). In addition, he did consultant work for many states that wanted to improve their institutional programs.

Summary and Conclusion

During the 1930-1940 period, the reform spirit of the 1901-1929 period was popularized and institutionalized. Almost every innovation of the period was linked directly to the quiet genius of Austin MacCormick. He led correctional education through the difficult times after Osborne's death, and established the basis of modern practice. His definitive book offered relevant advice on individualized and group instruction, he established the Correctional Education Association and its *Journal*, and had a hand in the implementation of the first correctional education bureaus in New York State and the Federal Bureau of Prisons. Just as the previous period was largely shaped by Osborne's personality, the 1930-1940 period was shaped by MacCormick's.

The 1941-1945 Period

Introduction

The nation's attention was focused on World War II. Prisons were transformed into factories to supply goods for the War—foodstuffs, boots, tents, and so forth. As always during war, many people who might otherwise have come in contact with the juvenile or criminal justice systems found themselves at the front, instead.

The same thing happened to correctional educators. The generation of leaders who had ushered in the Golden Years of the 1930-1940 period marched off to the front, and most of them never returned to their previous positions. This is the origin of the current amnesia experienced by correctional educators. The years since 1941 have largely been consumed with the struggle first to regain the systematic basis for the exemplary programs of the previous period (this lasted at least until the mid-1970s), and then to refine post-War gains (since about 1974 or 1976).

In general, studies indicated that school enrollment in reformatories was about twice that of prisons. Local school methods predominated. In New York State, where Glenn Kendall was in charge of prison education during the early part of this period, there were substantial improvements in cost analysis and cost projections. Austin MacCormick received the Presidential Medal of Honor for helping to plan the U.S. prisons in Asia during the War. The only real hot spot in correctional education was at a new facility in California. Even the *Journal of Correctional Education* discontinued publication for several years during this period.

Prisoners Are People

Reform warden Kenyon Scudder helped establish the California Institute for Men (CIM), in Chino in 1941, as a prison without walls. The title of his book *Prisoners are People* (1968/1952) summarizes his disposition toward the work. Scudder is known for managing CIM during World War II, and for (a) enthusiastically supporting prison industries that would contribute to the war effort, (b) founding the inmate forestry patrols that have contributed so much to fire abatement in the subsequent decades, and (c) facilitating the development of correctional education according to the same parameters that regulated local school education. Consistent with the maxim that educators should be in charge of educational decisions, he contracted with the Chino School District for teachers. This relationship has been carried into the present. The following passage describes its origins.

> We needed to provide regular courses from the first grade through high school, as nine per cent of men in prison had never learned to read or write and most of the others had dropped out of school early. I did not want to have inmate teachers [the

norm at that time], for that plan has never been successful in any prison. Neither did I want to take on a group of teachers full time. We decided to ask the high school district to sponsor the program on an average daily attendance basis as they did the high school and adult education classes in the community, they to furnish the teachers and we to provide the students and equipment. Soon after Chino opened, I called on my good friend, the late Dr. Walter Dexter, State Superintendent of Public Instruction in Sacramento. He immediately grasped the significance of our plan and thought it could be worked out, but when he called one of his department heads, he ran into opposition at once. 'This would be a dangerous precedent to establish,' the man said. 'If we approve it for Chino, San Quentin and Folsom will also want it, and there is no telling where it will end.' Dr. Dexter pressed a buzzer. 'Ask Mr. Lentz to come in,' he said. Mr. Lentz was legal adviser for the State Department of Education. 'I see no reason why the plan won't work,' Lentz said. 'It would be the same as an adult education program in any other community, with the school district reimbursed through the average daily attendance fund. There is no legal barrier to prevent the high school from taking the institution into its area.' Dr. Dexter concluded the conference by saying, 'If there is any group of men in the state that needs this training, it is our prisoners. Perhaps they would not now be in custody if the schools had given them better opportunities earlier in life.' The Chino Board of Education approved the establishment of day and evening vocational classes on the premises of...[CIM] under the direction of the Chino Board of Education. It permitted all instruction to be by civilian teachers fully certified by the State Board of Education, which meant that our men could therefore receive their graduation certificates from the Chino high school district instead of from a state prison. This has become a permanent arrangement... (Scudder, 1968/1952, pp. 149-150).

Summary and Conclusion

World War II diverted attention from correctional education. With the exception of a few improvements in New York and California, there was not much happening in our field during this period. Further, much of the energy that would be directed to regaining the status and proficiency of pre-World War II correctional education would preoccupy the field for several decades.

The 1946 to 1963 Period

Introduction

There is little to report about this historic period. "The golden years" of correctional education ended with World War II. In its aftermath the profession struggled to regain its balance, mostly without the leaders who had set the pace during the 1930 to 1940 period. MacCormick remained available for correctional educators, but most of his work was now directed to more fundamental prison reform issues. Many correctional educators were new to the field, unaware of the grand programs and scholarly work that had gone on before.

Themes of the Period

Some modern historians maintain that the period after World War II ushered in "the new industrial prison." From a correctional education perspective, however, the Auburn system had been an industrial or factory system, and no new systems of lasting importance were introduced during these immediate postwar years. The Auburn and Reformatory Prison Discipline systems had contained all the elements of the 1950s prison experience; it is therefore difficult to suggest that anything new emerged.

Glenn Kendall succeeded Walter Wallack as director of the New York State prison education. As soon as the War was over Kendall established an inmate reception center at Elmira. He had written one book on applications of the diagnostic-prescriptive method in correctional education, and another on social education—the definitive volume on that subject for decades, *The Organization and Teaching of Social and Economic Studies in Correctional Institutions* (1939). In other words, Kendall continued and extended both parts of MacCormick's work, on individualized and group work in correctional education.

The reception center was an attempt to apply a clinical approach, consistent with the new behavioral psychology, to the classification model that John Howard had recommended and Alexander Maconochie had implemented. It marked a critical juncture in the organization of what would later be called the medical model, and applied to corrections.

Norm-based testing had been implemented on a large scale in the Army during World War I, but it was not applied in most correctional institutions until after World War II. Classification was seen as the new frontier of corrections during this period, capable of revitalizing institutional programs. The concept was closely linked to work with "defective delinquents" (a term that often designated recidivists with a history of sexual crimes). The definition of defective delinquency varied from state to state and even from prison to prison. Kendall directed a great deal of study to the educational issues associated with incarcerated defective delinquents.

Price Chenault became the first Correctional Education Association (CEA) president in 1946. That was when the American Prison Association (APA) Standing Committee on Education adopted the CEA name, and moved from Standing Committee status to that of an APA affiliate. The CEA was becoming more independent. Chenault is remembered especially for his social education curricula, and for his articles on the history of inmate education in New York. He came after Glenn Kendall as New York State director of prison education.

Surplus World War II documentary films were used for social education classes. They were mostly on hygiene, good manners, work and family values, and how to avoid getting a social disease. Correctional educators emphasized group instruction. An important and enduring aspect of the correctional education curriculum, social education, was also a fad of the postwar period. Individualized instruction was largely neglected, despite the useful advice that MacCormick and Kendall had provided.

Summary and Conclusion

The themes of this period can be discussed almost like a list since there was so little happening. The renewed emphasis on prison industries was really a diluted continuation of wartime munitions production. Prison industries production did not increase after the War, but it seemed more important by default—because correctional education services were not growing at the same rate as the inmate population. The CEA entered the postwar period with greater clarity, officially distancing itself from the old guard of the APA. New York State's bureau still dominated correctional education. The new generation of correctional educators, many of whom were unfamiliar with MacCormick's balanced approach, aspired to establish a group social education format. Simultaneously, increased support was expressed for the medical model, and for an individualized, clinical or behavioral approach in general. The preliminary conditions were set for a major, profession-wide dialogue about whether correctional education should pursue the individualized or group instruction format.

The 1964 to 1980 Period

Introduction

This period began with the civil rights legislation that led almost directly to a new Federal emphasis on equal access to educational opportunity. It ended with the promised cutback in domestic spending, part of the conservative experience of the Reagan presidency.

There was hope that correctional education might regain the level of activity and stature it had enjoyed during the 1930-1940 period—but it did not. Correctional education was jump-started with Federal funds during the 1964-1980 period. However, the leadership quality of the pre-World War II period, with its twin emphases on vision and practicality, was lost. The result was almost as if a generation had been skipped. Most of the leaders were still alive, although they were no longer employed in correctional education. Most of the new incumbents were unschooled in their own profession, out of touch with the great literature of the previous epochs, and unable even to ask the right questions of previous leaders. The 1964 to 1980 period was marked by overcrowding and institutionalization; a few specific reforms were implemented, but they would not really assume center stage until long after this period was over.

Trends in Funding and Correctional School Districts

The Correctional Education Association (CEA) slowly gained momentum. CEA conferences were still components of American Correctional Association (ACA) congresses until the early 1970s, but the *Journal of Correctional Education* and the other groundwork that MacCormick had begun were producing important dividends. Tom Hageman served as CEA vice president, and then as president (1968-70). He was the state director of prison education in Missouri.

The Missouri correctional education operation took the bureau model to its highest threshold, consistent with the design that MacCormick and Roosevelt had originally conceptualized. Subsequent Missouri state directors of correctional education suggested the bureau actually functioned like a correctional school district, the modern state-of-the-art organizational model. However, the Missouri State Department of Education never extended all the rights and obligations of a school district to the Missouri correctional education system. Therefore, it can only be reported that the organization represented the highest development that a bureau can assume without actually becoming a school district.

There was growing concern during this period about how to access the new Federal funding programs for education. The "Big Three" programs were not typically available to correctional education: Adult Education (especially Title VI, Adult Basic Education), Vocational Education (now known as the Carl Perkins Act), and Title I, the No Child Left Behind Education Act.

Federal funds for special education only became available in 1975, and their application to correctional education was delayed considerably. Many states did not access special education monies until the early 1980s, and some have not accessed them yet. Instead, Federal funds for correctional education came from a matrix of programs. For a few years there were Vocational Rehabilitation funds, Teacher Corps funds, and Comprehensive Education and Training Act funds, all from Federal sources. However, despite access problems, the Big Three dominated Federal funding for correctional education.

The problem was that state departments of education were only allowed to "pass through" Federal funds to eligible school districts. Correctional education did not have any school districts during the mid-1960s, when the Federal government opened up important resources for education. Most states had adopted the popular correctional education bureau model, pioneered during the 1929-1941 years in the Federal Bureau of Prisons and New York State.

George Beto was the director of the Texas Department of Corrections. He sponsored a study which found that recidivism rates for inmates who had acquired at least six college credits were substantially reduced. In 1965 Beto established the Texas Prison College System. Through this highly visible and somewhat controversial action Beto demonstrated he was a friend to correctional education. The field's attention became focused on the Texas experiment.

In 1968 the Federal government acknowledged this innovation and established Project NewGate, named after the early prisons in London and New York City. Project NewGate was a comprehensive prison college program, complete with counseling and follow-up services. The best book on the subject is by Seashore and Haberfeld, *Prison Education* (1976). The rise of postsecondary education was an important part of correctional education during the 1964-1980 period. Although there were college programs in some states that pre-dated Texas', the increased attention on these programs led to increased respect for Texas correctional education.

Then in 1969 Beto established the first modern correctional school district, Texas Department of Corrections' Windham School District (now renamed Windham School System). Dr. Lane Murray was appointed Windham superintendent of schools. The funding advantage of the school district model during this period accrued mostly from its ability to access Federal monies for education directly through the State department of education (the Texas Education Agency). Windham established a leadership role in many aspects of correctional education. Many correctional educators today associate the school district concept with Texas prisons.

However, a correctional school district had been established in New Jersey in 1909, at Trenton State Prison. It functioned with special assistance from the State Department of Education, and implemented many improvements in the education program. The model was phased out in 1923, when New Jersey's Institutions and Agencies "superagency" became fully operational.

By the end of the 1964-1980 period there were nine statewide correctional school districts. The school district pattern was proclaimed the state-of-the-art cure for the access to funding dilemma. The American Bar Association, through its Clearinghouse for Offender Literacy, disseminated information, legislation, and draft legislation on the emerging school district pattern for lawmakers and lay advocates in its now famous Special Bulletins on the subject.

Many correctional educators see the correctional school district as a panacea for all the problems of correctional education. However, no model can live up to that expectation. The school district structure has the inherent advantage of making correctional education live up to all the tests of the local public schools—so correctional educators and students can look eye to eye with their local school counterparts. This advantage results from the correctional school district procedure that statewide statutory and regulatory requirements applying to regular school districts must apply to institutional schools. Though many of the standards can be articulated for application in a confinement setting, the impact of compliance with pertinent regulations can be a great boon to institutional teachers and students. In addition, correctional school district staff must be qualified according to the same standards that apply to local school district staff, including (and especially) the superintendent of schools. Together, these requirements tend to put educators in charge of correctional education, instead of institutional administrators who tend to be non-educators. That is a wonderful advantage, but it does not make correctional education immune to all the problems that regularly hinder teaching and learning in a complex and shifting social milieu.

Lane Murray served twice as CEA president. It was under her leadership, in 1974, that the first independent CEA national conference was implemented (it was no longer a component of the ACA congress). Murray was awarded the ACA's E.R. Cass Award, its highest honor, which has gone only to a few correctional educators, including MacCormick and Murray.

Some Issues of this Period

MacCormick attended the 1970 ACA conference. It was held in Cincinnati, the site of the 1870 conference that had ushered in the reformatory movement. One of the processes that began at the 1870 conference was the professionalization of corrections. The modern institutional accreditation movement emerged directly from this 1870 effort.

Accreditation standards regulate parameters of good institutional management, including facilities, staffing, inservice, and aspects of the education and library programs. In the last few years, the CEA has been active with its own set of education-relevant standards. One problem with these systems is that educators in the "outside" community may not be invested in the success of the ACA or CEA institutional standard systems. Instead, they focus on accreditation by their state department of education, and especially by their regional association of schools and colleges.

A second problem is that the standards themselves have focused on quantitative guidelines for good institutional management. These guidelines are generally appropriate, but there are important qualitative dimensions of education that require attention, as well. For example, ACA standards are specific with regard to the placement of fire extinguishers and some of the architectural requirements of a school, but they are not directly applicable to conditions that encourage or discourage learning and teaching. Some fully accredited institutional school programs are staffed with correctional educators who emphasize their own careers instead of student learning.

The dynamics of institutional education diverge qualitatively from those of the local schools. Because of the intensity of correctional education, many staff members have become flashes in the pan, or gotten discouraged, or have given up the teaching/learning struggle to become collaborators (in the wartime sense) with anti-education, institutional administrators.

One pattern of negative collaboration exists when the education leader looks to the non-educator administrator for education leadership. This problem emerges whenever one department denies its own function (i.e., education) and retreats in favor of another (security or prison industry). This default is an inevitable legacy of institutionalized systems—and it frequently does not show up during the accreditation process.

The innovative correctional education models that were pursued in Texas were one part this period's drama. The Texas Department of Corrections frequently identified itself as the last Auburn system corrections department in the nation. Texas prisons were constructed in rings around Huntsville, which is known as the prison capital of Texas, for easy access by Statewide prison administrators.

In Windham School District academic students attended school once a week, for five hours. Windham vocational students attended school five days a week. The Windham School District Board had the same membership as the Texas Department of Corrections Board. A major class-action suit by inmates against Texas Department of Corrections in 1975, known as the *Ruiz v. Estelle* case, resulted in substantial improvements in the Windham service delivery system, especially in the area of special education. Jim Estelle was the Texas Department of Corrections director who succeeded George Beto.

Another trend of the 1964-1980 period was the emergence in the early 1970s of University-based correctional teacher preparation programs. The first programs were founded as a result of needs identified by local corrections and university leaders, and each one had a different focus. For example, the Western Illinois University program emphasized elementary education content; the Coppin State College (Maryland) program emphasized adult basic education; the Lehigh University (Pennsylvania) program emphasized counseling and special education; the Sam Houston University (Texas) program emphasized criminal justice; the Memphis State University (Tennessee) program emphasized general rehabilitative services, but staff there did not really identify with correctional education; the University of Virginia program emphasized special education. Collectively, these are known as first generation correctional teacher preparation programs. Dr. Joe Kersting (Western Illinois) and Dr. Ray Bell (Lehigh) became leaders in correctional education as a result of their salient and sustained contributions in the area of teacher preparation.

Second and third generation correctional teacher education programs were introduced during the subsequent period. Second generation programs were funded with special education monies for personnel development, and third generation programs are eclectic—structured to correspond with the eclectic nature of the field of correctional education.

Some of the Main Contributors

One of the main contributors during this period was Dr. T.A. Ryan, who taught at the University of Hawaii and recently retired, professor emeritus, from the University of South Carolina at Columbia. Focusing on systems applications in correctional adult and career education, Ryan's work was represented, in part, in the Educational Resources Information Center (ERIC) microfiche system. Her inservice efforts, monograph on programs for female offenders, and program evaluation projects have been a source of great encouragement and help to many field-based correctional educators across the country.

Dr. John McKee's work at Draper Correctional Institution, in Elmore, Alabama was a lasting contribution to correctional education. During the 1960s and '70s McKee was one of the pioneers in individualized instruction, especially with the new generation of teaching machines and diagnostic tests. At one point, McKee developed a test that can be used to predict recidivism, *The Environmental Deprivation Scale* (Jenkins, 1972). He has a whole line of relevant correctional education products he has conceptualized, implemented, and marketed. At least one of Alabama's prisons became racially integrated during the mid-1960s in order to qualify for a vocational education grant that Dr. McKee obtained. McKee's contribution is related to the advice MacCormick left in his book, about how to do individualized correctional education classroom activities. In fact, McKee and MacCormick were friends.

On another front, in the 1960s, CEA president Tom Hageman launched a series of negotiations with the National Education Association (NEA), aimed at organizational affiliation. As NEA moved closer to union status during the late 1960s and early 1970s, this affiliation might have opened a new path for correctional education in many states. However, the CEA leadership group did not endorse the concept, and the affiliation with the American Correctional Association was maintained as the CEA's sole, formalized relationship, although some have since been added.

Tony DelPopolo, Jr. served as CEA president after Tom Hageman. He lived in Virginia, and coordinated the Washington, D.C. Jail education program at Lorton. DelPopolo chronicled many of the correctional education advances during this period. He also implemented the CEA regional structure. The regional boundaries have been adjusted since then, but the basic concept is still operational. There were many other heroes of correctional education during this period, but these contributions were most relevant to our current tasks.

The Arkansas Debacle

The Texas and Arkansas Departments of Corrections kept convicts occupied, in part, with labor on road and work gangs. They also used the Plummer System, so named because was designed in Delaware by a man named Plummer. This cost-saving procedure put inmates in charge of other inmates, as officers. At some Arkansas facilities trustee officers were armed. Reasonable food and medical services were available for a fee. Conditions in Arkansas during this period resembled those that John Howard had encountered in English gaols about the time of the American Revolution.

Tom Murton, who had been a corrections official in Alaska, was assigned as warden of the Arkansas Cummins Farm unit. Murton was critical of Austin MacCormick. He saw him as part of the prison management establishment, and therefore substantially responsible for prison brutality. Murton apparently did not see himself in that role. Tom Murton announced that he would improve on Thomas Mott Osborne's Mutual Welfare League system. This initiative would be parallel to Howard Gill's 1930s failed program in Massachusetts. Indeed, evidence suggests Murton and Gill might have been in touch with each other. As part of his plan, Murton sought to involve guards and other staff in the democratic organization. (Readers should note that, although Murton was ultimately unable to implement this change, it was successfully implemented at Barlinnie Prison in Scotland in the 1980s.)

The Robert Redford movie *Brubaker* was a stylized version of Murton's Arkansas career, except that the part about his voluntary incarceration was borrowed from Thomas Mott Osborne's life. Murton made important changes at Cummins Farm. He introduced a democratic management procedure, improved the school, reversed the terrible problems that had grown from the Plummer System, and hired female teachers.

However, when Murton discovered the remains of inmates who had been tortured to death at Cummins Farm under the authority of previous wardens, and publicized the event, Arkansas governor Winthrop Rockefeller had him put under house arrest. There is a famous picture of Murton with a bag full of human remains dug up from the prison grounds. Murton was soon fired. His side of this story is told in his book *Accomplices to the Crime: The Arkansas Prison Scandal* (1969). Another interesting book he wrote is *The Dilemma of Prison Reform* (1976). After his career in Arkansas ended, Murton established a duck farm in Oklahoma.

However, before leaving the corrections business entirely, Tom Murton started a prison reform newsletter that raised salient issues and questions. It criticized prisons as bastions of hate and prejudice, prison reform as a field of great fanfare but few useful programs, and prison procedures as substantially unchanged during the last 200 years.

Chapters from *The Education of Adult Prisoners*

Most modern correctional educators have not had the opportunity to read MacCormick's definitive 1931 book, *The Education of Adult Prisoners*. Nevertheless, some correctional education leaders had access During the 1964-1980 period, problems resulted from overemphasizing parts of MacCormick's program, while neglecting other parts. These problems have many aspects. Three of the most important aspects resulted from neglect of MacCormick's balanced program, which included (a) both basic and cultural education, (b) adult education for the development of the whole person, and (c) both individualized and group instruction. The narrowing of the rich, comprehensive legacy left by MacCormick is outlined in the next paragraphs.

The theme of cultural education in corrections has frequently been ignored by American correctional educators, despite the popularity of humanities education in prisons located in Canada, Ireland, and other European countries. MacCormick made a good case for cultural education in his 1931 book. During the current period (1989-the present) the humanities issue has gained increased currency. However, it was quite often neglected during the 1964-1980 period.

Another of MacCormick's themes that was inappropriately adjusted was adult education. MacCormick intended that this aspect of correctional education would include education in its broadest sense, to put inmate students in touch with the scope of modern knowledge. Instead, many correctional educators focused entirely on basic academic and marketable skills. Thus, MacCormick's grand concept of adult education in corrections became institutionalized as mere adult basic education, often with content patterned on the basic skills training of elementary children in the local schools.

During the 1964-1980 period Malcolm Knowles was a key leader of adult education; indeed, his role was similar to MacCormick's role in correctional education. In his book *The Modern Practice of Adult Education* (1970), Knowles coined the term "andragogy" (adult education), as opposed to "pedagogy" (the education of children). As an expression of the movement away from "basic skills only" in adult education, Knowles wrote "Farewell to pedagogy." This phrase resonated with meaning for adult educators who were not involved in correctional education, but its import seems to have been incomprehensible to institutionalized teachers in corrections. By focusing on only one part of MacCormick's adult education theme in corrections, correctional educators were reducing a noble profession to a mere institutional program.

Another problem of the 1964-1980 period was that teachers in juvenile institutions were sometimes reluctant to identify professionally with correctional education. This issue had several roots. One was that juvenile institution staff often did not want to identify their work with the harsh realities of prisons. Instead, juvenile teachers tended to identify professionally with public schools and related, content-oriented disciplines (English, math, and so forth), rather than with correctional education.

MacCormick had introduced the adult education paradigm into correctional education in such a way that its could be selectively implemented in juvenile institutions. In addition, the school district model, which had been piloted in modern times in Texas prisons, had widest currency in adult systems. For these reasons and others, the modern correctional education movement has been dominated by adult prison education staff. Many juvenile institution educators remain extremely cautious about the term "correctional education." Nevertheless, fully one third of CEA membership is from juvenile institutions, and the parallels between institutional adult and juvenile education are extensive. On the whole, the element of confinement is a great leveler. In the face of this common variable, differences of age and types of offense are relatively unimportant.

A final problem that resulted from narrow application of parts of MacCormick's program was the issue of whether correctional education should use the individualized or group format for teaching and learning. The professional dialogue associated with this question dominated the field of correctional education during the 1964-1980 period. Indeed, aftershocks of that dialogue lingered long into the 1980s.

This issue reflected professional interpretations of the correctional education mission. Would the social education emphasis of the 1946-1963 period, with its concern about inmate values and attitudes, be extended into the 1964-1980 period? Or would the individualized education emphasis, with its renewed focus on inmate literacy and occupational skills, be highlighted? The correctional education community was extremely divided on this subject. If they had access to MacCormick's book, correctional educators might have taken his advice and applied both modalities, using each to help meet the whole student's needs. As it played out, however, the field gradually moved toward the individualized approach and usually applied it reductionistically—to the near exclusion of grouped learning opportunities. Eventually the profession aspired to exclude group instruction totally. This shift led to the "skills only" pattern that would characterize much of correctional education instruction during the next period, from 1981-1988.

Summary and Conclusion

During the 1964-1980 period the correctional education field was beginning to pick up the pieces that had been scattered as a result of the Second World War. Correctional education lost its zeal. The players had changed, an authoritarian model dominated, reform efforts were marginal—more like adjustments or accommodations than meaningful reforms, and in some states the press of overcrowding was starting to acquire the magnitude that would later characterize the current period. Nevertheless, important trends would unfold from this state of affairs. The CEA was gradually becoming consolidated again, some correctional teacher education programs became operational, postsecondary programs were being established, some new Federal monies were available, and the school district organizational pattern was welcomed by the field. Parts of MacCormick's legacy were emphasized over other parts, but the balanced program he had recommended was simply not to be found in the field or addressed as a whole in any single book or report. This was a transitional period, in which some of the features that we associate with modern correctional education became identifiable.

The 1981-1988 Period

Introduction

Many observers of correctional education believe that the conservative years of the Reagan presidency, with its cutbacks in domestic spending and "tough on crime" community attitudes, necessarily resulted in a retreat of correctional education. This belief is not supported by the facts. If retrenchment necessarily resulted in withdrawal, the 1930s would have been the time of greatest retreat. However, as we have seen the "law and order" Great Depression period of correctional education was one of the most productive epochs. Similarly, despite many setbacks in correctional education during the 1980s, the 1981-1988 period was a time of limited progress.

The chief arenas of this progress were the new correctional school districts, university-based correctional teacher preparation programs, the Correctional Education Association, and the U.S. Education Department. Secondary sources of support were the emerging special education community, Supreme Court Chief Justice Warren Burger's advocacy of prison education, a new wave of correctional education-specific literature, and some other unexpected quarters. The 1980s were not a happy time for the field—many states and local jurisdictions experienced intermittent funding patterns that wreaked havoc for correctional educators and correctional education. Nevertheless, many incumbents had the sense the profession was finally resurging from the battering it had sustained during the World War II period.

The 1981-1988 period was largely driven by the pressures of overcrowding, and the resultant search for funding. Reform itself became institutionalized. Gone were the controversial initiatives of Zebulon Brockway, Thomas Mott Osborne, and Katherine Bement Davis. Instead, correctional education reforms were planned by professionals who behaved as if their knowledge of social change strategies was limited to the top-down approach. Correctional education, caught up entirely in the dynamics of the authoritarian and materialistic Cold War cultural milieu, had itself become institutionalized.

Some of the Contributors

John Erwin was appointed chaplain at Chicago's Cook County Jail in the mid-1950s. By the early 1980s he had an eight million dollar correctional education budget, was a presidential appointee to the National Advisory Council on Vocational Education, and had gained national prominence for his PACE initiative, Programmed Adult Correctional Education. The PACE program curriculum and procedures were based on Dr. John McKee's contributions to the field, which were introduced in the narrative about 1964-1980 period.

Reverend John Erwin had been a juvenile delinquent. His personal stories about how he was treated as an offender, and how educators helped him transform his life, frequently won intense support from audiences of correctional teachers. He wrote a popular book called, *The Man Who Keeps Going to Jail*, in 1978. After his PACE involvement, Erwin worked as a volunteer in the program led by Chuck Colson (of Watergate fame).

Dr. Richard Carlson was a main player in the establishment of the U.S. Education Department's Corrections Program. He was assigned to the National Institute for Education and worked closely with the National Advisory Council on Vocational Education, along with John Erwin. Carlson implemented a nationwide survey on vocational education in corrections, and a series of participatory regional hearings on the subject. He was a great supporter of the correctional school district organization structure. Carlson helped mobilize National Institute for Corrections funds to implement the Corrections Program in the U.S. Education Department, and supervised that program for a time.

In 1978 the U.S. Congress had passed the Correctional Education Demonstration Act. President Carter never spent the money that was assigned for that purpose. At about the same time, a consultant firm named Metametrix announced that there were approximately 70 Federal funding programs applicable to correctional education, but that the Federal government had no coordination of its correctional education initiatives. The Correctional Education Association directed a great deal of effort to the task of advocating the establishment of an appropriately visible and influential office to provide the needed services.

Former CEA president Bob Terhune of Ohio got U.S. presidential candidate Jimmy Carter to promise that, in the event that a U.S. Education Department was established during his presidency, it would include a Corrections Desk. As one of Carter's last efforts in the White House, the Education Department was established, and a CEA team under Dr. Richard Carlson launched the proposals that resulted in Corrections Program implementation. This was an important initiative.

In the 19th century Sarah Martin (a contemporary of Elizabeth Fry) was known as "the prisoners' friend." At about the middle of the 20th century the head of correctional education in England and Wales, C.T. Cape, was known as "the teachers' friend." During the 1980s Senator Claiborne Pell of Rhode Island was known as a friend of correctional education. Pell was steadfast in his advocacy of correctional education consolidation and improvement. The funding assistance program for postsecondary students (formerly Basic Educational Opportunity Grants) was renamed in his honor—Pell Grants.

During the 1981-1988 period, research findings had revealed that there were approximately 20,000 correctional educators in the state, local, Federal, and private institutions across the country. Several nationwide surveys described the problems they encountered in their various institutional assignments: poor facilities, lack of resources, infrequent supervisory support, intermittent program evaluation, alienated or embittered learners, few correctional education teacher preparation programs, an amorphous professional identity, and so forth. However, one of the issues that was raised most frequently was that—regardless of who employed them—the correctional teachers were often treated as strangers in the institution, and looked down upon by other staff members.

Bo Lozoff emphasized another dimension of correctional education, the inherent spiritual potential of the incarceration experience. He encouraged offenders to use their time behind bars like a monks use time in a monastery. His prison work began at the Federal Correctional Institution at Butner, North Carolina. Lozoff's primary organizations for this purpose were the Prison Ashram Project (an ashram is a monastery), the Human Kindness Foundation, and a rock music group he organized. Lozoff's 1976 book *Inside Out* is a spiritual guide for prisoners; his most popular book during the 1980s was *We're All Doing Time* (1985).

As the period wore on, increasing concern was directed to the problem of idle time for inmates. Known as "the warden's bane," idle time frequently results in assaults and escape plans. The solution to the idle time problem, of course, was education. Two types of conservatives gained prominence during the 1981-1988 period; they can be characterized by the terms entrepreneurial and traditional. Entrepreneurial conservatives were reluctant to support correctional education because money invested in institutional programs never realized short-term dividends. Traditionalists, however, tended to support correctional education because it helped institutional superintendents cope with idle time, while sustaining traditional values. Always true to the law and order ideology, traditional conservatives generally advocated whatever wardens needed to keep control over confined populations. They therefore tended to support correctional education.

One of the primary contributors to the high profile that correctional education maintained during this period was U.S. Supreme Court Chief Justice Warren Burger. He gave many speeches about recidivism and the need to help convicted felons leave the prisons in better shape than they entered. This made good sense, and was inherently appealing to conservatives and liberals. He repeatedly emphasized the theme of "learning one's way out of prison," and the central role of correctional education in institutional programming. One of the Chief Justice's special projects was the TIE approach to academic and vocational linkages—Training, Industries, and Education. A spin-off of this attention was the Free Venture Program, a Federally sponsored initiative to bring outside entrepreneurs "inside," offering competitive employment with relatively decent, minimum wages for confined workers. A portion of their earnings was directed to room and board, victims' programs, and savings for their ultimate release.

The TIE approach was popular among Correctional Education Association leaders. The CEA was managed by several presidents from Texas who helped to hold the organization together through much of the 1980s, and then by a series of presidents who worked to consolidate CEA committee structures. During the 1930s the CEA established its first statewide affiliate organizations, embarked on its Resolutions and CEA Accreditation efforts, founded the President's Council and the Special Interest Group structure, and in many ways maintained the professionalization focus envisioned by its founder, Austin MacCormick.

Nevertheless, something had changed. The profession was making great advances while teacher vitality seemed to wane. Management issues continued to dominate ever more strongly; MacCormick's student learning focus was less evident. A new generation of leaders had emerged. CEA was becoming institutionalized.

This was the period when Dr. Osa Coffey began her full-time nationwide correctional education career as the coordinator of the U.S. Education Department's Corrections Program under Dr. Richard Carlson. Then she became the first CEA executive director, and was later assigned superintendent of schools for Virginia's correctional school district. Dr. Coffey was succeeded in the U.S. Education Department by Dr. Dianne Carter, who went on to work at the National Institute of Corrections Training Academy in Boulder Colorado. There were several interim incumbents in the U.S. Education Department Corrections Program during the late 1980s. John Linton presently holds this position.

Correctional School Districts and University-Based Correctional Teacher Preparation Programs

By 1988 there were 19 statewide correctional school districts: in the Alabama youth system, Arizona youth, Arkansas adult, Connecticut youth, Connecticut adult, Florida adult, Illinois youth and adult, Maryland adult, New Jersey youth and adult, Ohio youth, Ohio adult, South Carolina youth, South Carolina adult, Tennessee youth, Tennessee adult, Texas adult, Vermont adult, Virginia youth and adult, and the West Virginia youth and adult system. The emphasis on state discretionary authority in the use of Federal funds for education during the Reagan presidency neutralized the need to implement the school district structure to improve access to Federal funds. In fact, during the period of domestic cutbacks, per student expenditures for correctional school districts were not statistically different from those of the old correctional education bureaus. Correctional education in many states was successfully accessing Federal support without the school district structure. Instead, states were now deciding to implement the state-of-the-art correctional school district organization pattern in order to improve the quality of institutional education. This change helped to balance other negative trends, to keep alive the enthusiasm for professionalization.

These 19 states used a variety of funding strategies, but the traditional line item budget dominated all funding procedures. Many of the new school districts developed impressive records of instructional innovation. In a period of intense and relatively unpredictable budget cuts, the school districts were on average more successful than the old bureaus in warding off cuts that undermined the program. A new emphasis on professional leadership emerged, and the state directors of correctional education established their own professional and political organization, which sometimes functioned as a subgroup of the CEA. The new school districts became beacons for increased professionalization.

It had taken decades for the school district pattern of organization to get implemented "inside." Secure and consolidated in the local public schools by the turn of the century, the modern correctional school district movement had only penetrated to state institutions in the late 1960s. The changing emphasis from funding access as the only acceptable rationale to an emphasis on program quality was seen as compelling to many in the field. The school district organizational pattern was increasingly used as a strategy for putting educators in charge of institutional education decisions, especially in the areas of curriculum, budget, and personnel. During the 1981-1988 period, however, its dissemination was so slow that many correctional educators became disheartened.

Another new source of support was the growth of a second generation of university- or college-based correctional teacher preparation programs. Readers will recall that first generation programs had emerged during the 1964-1980 period, based on divergent and locally identified needs. Second generation programs were prompted by the availability of Federal special education funds. They were located at Southern Illinois University, Slippery Rock University (PA), the University of Maryland, Lenoir-Rhyne College (NC), State University of New York (New Paltz), and George Washington University (Washington, D.C.). Some special education advocates and faculty from these programs surmised that correctional education is special education in an institutional setting. This was not entirely true, since most confined students were not educationally disabled, and all categories of learners may be found inside. In addition, correctional education is a field of education, with its own history and literature apart from special education. Despite this issue, second generation teacher preparation programs provided a new source of scholarship and identity for the growing field of correctional education.

Education for Incarcerated Learners with Disabilities

Ever since the 1954 *Brown v. Board* decision that ushered in the age of desegregation, equality of educational opportunity has been an underlying aspiration of American education. Public Law (PL) 94-142, the Education of All Handicapped Children Act and associated legislation, IDEA, was properly seen in this context. Special education is designed to reach students who formerly did not receive equal access, and PL 94-142 specified that it was available to students wherever they were located, including corrections.

The prototypes of many modern special education programs for educationally disabled students had been implemented at Zebulon Brockway's Elmira and other reformatories before the turn of the century. Special education in correctional institutions had been an important and longstanding issue.

Special Education in the Criminal Justice System (1987), by Nelson, Rutherford, and Wolford was the most comprehensive modern book on this subject. In general, concerns were raised about legal requirements of PL 94-142, the special applications to corrections, and about how correctional education systems could properly implement the Act. Special education used diagnostic-prescriptive procedures similar to those MacCormick had recommended, even though he applied them from an adult education perspective and did not apply modern identifying factors.

Emergence of a New Correctional Education Literature

As attention was brought to bear on the correctional education literature several problems emerged. Foremost among these was the lack of secondary sources (summarizing major trends). In addition, most of the best materials on correctional education had been out of print for years. Nevertheless, the 1981-1988 period ushered in substantial development of correctional education theory. The *Journal of Correctional Education* increasingly published articles on the professional identity of correctional educators, and on the history of the profession. In 1981 John Braithwaite, a former editor of that *Journal*, introduced his theories of greater and lesser eligibility in a book about Australian correctional education, *Prisons, Education, and Work*.

The theory of lesser eligibility holds that confined offenders, being guilty of crime, should not have privileges that accrue to the lowest strata of the working poor. According to this idea, educational opportunities should not be available to incarcerates, except for minimal programs that are absolutely required by law. Any other policy would make institutions attractive, and people would try to get sentenced and stay confined so they could benefit from the advantages of life "inside."

The theory of greater eligibility, on the other hand, holds that people become offenders because society took advantage of them. For example, children who grow up to be offenders might suffer from a poor home environment, inadequate schools, and poverty or its correlates (racism, sexism, frustrated expectations, lack of self esteem, exposure to drugs and vice, and so forth). Therefore, society owes them an opportunity to make up for these deficits. This theory holds that institutional education programs should be as extensive and effective as possible.

The 1981-1988 period was marked by the dichotomy represented by Braithwaite's two theories, rather than by either of the theories, per se. Most correctional educators thought of confined learners as either victimizers or as victims. It was not until the current period that thoughtful correctional educators began to realize that both the theory of lesser eligibility and the theory of greater eligibility contained grains of truth. According to this balanced view, criminals would be seen as both victimizers and victims. Each offender's case should be sorted out individually to determine which, or in what combination, the two theories apply.

During the 1981-1988 period the dichotomy resulted in vast curricular implications. Those who maintained confined learners were victimizers emphasized the "basic and marketable skills only" approach. Those who maintained that confined learners were victims sought to develop "the whole student." This issue would not be addressed with clarity until the current period, when many correctional educators began to realize that the students in their classes were both victimizers and victims, with many individual differences.

Summary and Conclusion

The 1981-1988 period brought correctional education closer to the limelight, with a national CEA headquarters, a special office in the U.S. Education Department, a proliferation of correctional school districts and correctional teacher preparation programs, and a U.S. Supreme Court Chief Justice who campaigned for correctional education. However, many of these victories seemed too abstract and intangible for correctional educators, who faced the profound challenge of periodic budget cuts, alienation from many other institutional departments, and the constrained environment fostered by "tough on crime" public sentiment and anti-education institutional staffs. This was clearly a mixed, difficult period for the field of correctional education.

The Current Period, 1989 to the Present

Introduction

This period was anticipated by a cluster of events that emphasized holistic and ecological thinking in correctional education. It was spurred on by the 1988 Correctional Education Association Region VII Vancouver Conference and the 1990 Vancouver International CEA Conference.

This narrative is part report, part forecast. To synthesize events that are still unfolding is a high-risk effort which should be measured more by approximation than precision. The exemplars of the current period, its specific events, and trends are in process and cannot be known with clarity. Nevertheless, many of the general directions and goals of the period can be portrayed with relative confidence.

Some researchers have sought to explain correctional education history through its connections with technology; prison industries; common schools, Dewey's progressivism, and special education; the growth of institutional treatment modalities; or the constraining effects of the law and order/tough on crime perspective. All these schemes make sense, and establish believable contexts for certain parts of correctional education history.

There is another perspective, however, which tends to offer more comprehensive explanations by linking correctional education with global events and trends. According to this standard, the field began at about the time of the French Revolution; the emancipation of slaves, and the quick pace of industrialism, immigration, and feminism during the last quarter of the 19th century catapulted the field forward; the world wars interrupted its progress; the authoritarian Cold War resulted in its clinical context; and the end of the Cold War offers promise of a new beginning, based on cultural aspirations that were postponed by hot and cold wars.

The latter view shaped this summary. According to this approach the current (culture period) agenda is to neutralize, undo, or reverse Cold War trends that negatively impacted correctional education. A present challenge for correctional educators is to interpret and apply recent international lessons: "think globally, act locally." How can the field benefit from the collapse of the Berlin Wall, the Cold War, and the Soviet Union? What domestic challenges can be addressed if excessive military expenditures from the War on Terror wind down? What are our aspirations, and can they be attained during this new and potentially positive epoch?

From this perspective, several culture period agenda items loom large. Correctional educators should expect that (a) learning will be redefined as "the ability to make ethical decisions," (b) correctional education will be redefined as an outreach and intervention strategy, (c) developmental education patterns will replace incremental instruction, (d) educators will gain more authority over educational decisions within the institutions, (e) the what works/best practices formula will increasingly shape correctional education preservice and inservice, (f) a new focus will emerge on internationalism (the antidote for provincialism and the bane of good-old-boys and girls) that will help empower correctional educators. However, (g) there is evidence that the institutional anti-education sentiment has been popularized among key decision-makers throughout the culture(s) at large, and (h) the cost of war (COW), a negative cultural element, has gradually displaced many expenditures of a more positive nature—education, health care, and investments in other nurturing and cultural programs. In short, many extremely positive processes are unfolding, but the overall cultural experience is very mixed and constrained, and most community members are experiencing great anxiety and frustration. Additional changes will no doubt become discernible, but these eight agenda items are all that the current writers will venture to predict at this time.

The Humanities Theme

In the early 1970s Canadians from the Penitentiary Service put together an integrated correctional education intervention model. It included theories from the U.K., U.S., and Israel, and suggested vast improvements that could be implemented over the "basic academic and marketable skills only" emphasis that was popular in the United States and Canada at the time. The new model included five major parts: a cognitive psychology base, cognitive-moral development, participatory management, a theory of the criminal personality, and a focus on learning in the humanities subjects. Over the years, the focus on the humanities gradually came to be seen as a label or theme that encapsulated this entire mix.

All Canadian correctional educators did not pursue the model in their classrooms. However, many Canadian correctional educators were informed about the model, and aspired to implement it in their classroom, school, or system. In this context, the term *humanities instruction* became a cue or euphemism for the entire five parts of the model.

The integrated Canadian correctional education model was most clearly articulated in Robert Ross' and Elizabeth Fabiano's 1985 book *Time to Think*. This was and is the definitive book of the current (culture) period, despite the fact that it appeared before the period actually began. Ross and Fabiano used a "what works?" approach. Their book could be summarized in the questions, "What works, and why?" And, "What does not work, and why?" These questions struck at the heart of the "nothing works" logic advanced by Martinson's 1974 review of the rehabilitative programs literature, and which Martinson later retracted. Ross and Fabiano maintained that Martinson's instruments were not sensitive enough to measure progress, that correctional education should apply an array of strategies if it is to reach various types of confined persons, that those strategies should be directed at the cognitive development of students (especially to increase interpersonal skills), and that a repertoire of successful programs is available to anyone who will take the time to study them.

Notice how Ross and Fabiano's conclusion—that successful programs are already operational and ready to be replicated—diverges so profoundly from MacCormick's earlier conclusion that no model programs were in place. These divergent conclusions suggest that progress has been experienced in correctional education, even though the pace often seems frustrating. The Federal Penitentiary Service of Canada and various universities were at the lead in humanities-oriented improvement efforts. However, they were not alone.

Wherever correctional educators struggled to transcend the classroom management mode, with its institutionalized emphases on paperwork, individualization, and incremental or programmed learning, the culture period agenda was advancing. In the United States, the showcase Westville Correctional Institution (IN), the school program managed by Dr. Shannon Ref, had a repertoire of culture period programs. The Arts in Corrections Program, liberal arts postsecondary programs, and inmate periodicals are all part of the modern effort. Teachers were part of this agenda when they applied whole-language reading activities, expanded on traditional social education and cultural program formats, or broke out of linear/fragmented curriculum constraints with whole-student oriented teaching and learning.

David Werner's 1990 book *Correctional Education: Theory and Practice* was an excellent handbook for those who taught confined students. Werner's perspective was part and parcel of the new agenda. Another part was the interdisciplinary approach to learning suggested by the new emphasis on *street law*. Various legal education materials were introduced that incorporated this highly motivational content. Perhaps the most accessible and useful street law system was fostered by the American Bar Association.

In 1989 the old correctional education handbook concept, which was begun in the 1940s but interrupted by America's entry into World War II, was re-established. This resurgence began under the leadership of Dr. Steve Duguid, the leading Canadian correctional education program contributor. Since then *The Yearbook of Correctional Education* was edited by Dr. Carolyn Eggleston at California State University, and then Dr. Stan Karcz of the University of Minnesota. Its success was a major indicator of the state of correctional education, and of the field's vitality during the early part of the current period. The *Yearbook* has appeared sporadically in recent years.

Duguid managed several postsecondary programs at institutions in British Columbia, from Simon Fraser University, near Vancouver. These programs were known for their emphasis on learning in the humanities and social sciences, and for their participatory management style. The literature is replete with materials by Duguid and about the Simon Fraser University program. That literature is especially helpful to correctional education advocates who seek to implement culture period programs.

One of his major theoretical contributions has been labeled "Duguid's synthesis." It describes two views of correctional education. The incremental view of correctional education is consistent with the diagnostic-prescriptive method, in which students study prescribed learning content in small doses, to enhance the perception of success. Incremental content is external to the student, and tends to consist of basic academic and marketable skills. The content is always fragmented and noncontroversial.

By contrast, the developmental view is relevant to cognitive, cognitive-moral, or cognitive-democratic student growth. Student maturation (with a focus on internally-meaningful learning) is encouraged through humanities and social sciences content. Ethical decision-making, critical thinking, and interpersonal skills are byproducts of this process, which often makes use of relatively controversial learning content. Access to humanities content does not mean that students in developmental programs do not study basic and marketable skills—it is a matter of expanded curricular scope, rather than the exclusion of basic content. The difference between incremental and developmental views suggests the demarcation between the "old" and "new" correctional education paradigms.

Dr. Joan Fulton, a Virginia cognitivist whose work with low achievers is relevant to correctional education, has advanced a three-stage summary of the history of teaching, which is parallel to Duguid's synthesis. We call it "Fulton's synthesis." In this model, classroom discipline predates Duguid's incremental learning. Discipline is based on teacher control of the learning situation, and emphasizes rote memorization, repetitive drill, and teacher authority/student subservience. Fulton's classroom management stage is analogous to Duguid's incremental view, and her instruction stage is analogous to Duguid's developmental view.

Still another culture period model was put forth in advance of the current period, and was not designed for application in correctional education. This model was designed by Brazilian educator Paulo Freire, and discussed in his books *Pedagogy of the Oppressed* (2001), and *Education for Critical Consciousness* (2005). Freire's "banking concept" is similar to Fulton's classroom discipline stage. Banking concept teachers never let go of their authority over classroom interactions—they act, and the students are acted upon; they are the font of all knowledge. The teacher invests knowledge in the students—hence the term "banking concept." Freire's equivalent to Duguid's developmental view and Fulton's instruction stage is known as the "problem posing method," in which the teacher facilitates student participation in the education process. Problem posing teachers help students identify curriculum content in which they are interested, conduct relevant research, and make sure the content is learned. According to this model the teacher is a classroom participant who assumes a back seat role, so the other participants (students) can take some responsibility for their own education.

Together, the ideas of Duguid, Fulton, and Freire address many aspects of the "new correctional education paradigm" of the culture period. These ideas are entirely consistent with the reform pattern emphasized by Maconochie,

Crofton, and Brockway; and with the democracy/citizenship pattern emphasized by George, Osborne, MacCormick, and Makarenko. The challenge for student growth during the current period can be summarized in the words: social maturation, personal responsibility, and participatory management.

Views about literacy have gone full circle in the last several years. Historically, literacy was denied to the dangerous classes, as indicated in the legal record. Peasants, women, African Americans, and confined criminals were systematically denied access to literacy. In some of the historic literature from England, offenders were actually referred to as the dangerous class, or the scum of the populace. By any traditional standard, then, literacy should be systematically denied to incarcerated students. This contrasts markedly with the current emphasis on literacy in correctional education.

Further, the record indicates that literacy was historically perceived as a tool subject, a "floor" upon which further education could be based. Today literacy is frequently perceived as a "ceiling" instead, and there is a great deal of discussion about making literacy instruction mandatory for convicts. Culture period correctional educators may profit by discarding these views and replacing them with a more comprehensive orientation toward literacy, to include cultural literacy.

The Correctional School District Issue

The progress of the school district model since 1969 was discussed in the summary narratives associated with the 1964-1980 and 1981-1988 periods. It is likely that this progress will continue during the culture period. However, the dynamics of the current period suggest yet another, and as yet overlooked advantage of the school district organizational pattern.

Readers will recall that the initial advantage associated with the correctional school district pattern (during the 1964-1980 period) was financial. School districts could directly access Federal funds that were passed through state education agencies—funds that could only be assigned to eligible organizations (school districts). Then, in the face of domestic spending cutbacks and pervasive deregulation, the most cited advantage of the school district pattern shifted to quality programming opportunities. School districts have more comprehensively staffed quality program capabilities than the earliest decentralized and subsequent bureau models. All three models are currently operational, often in adjacent states.

During the current culture period a third major advantage of the correctional school district model will be identified—one that clarifies and extends the previously cited advantages. This one is based on the staff aspiration to implement developmental teaching and learning, systemwide.

In the often laissez-faire instructional systems inherent in the decentralized and bureau administrative models, there may be few impediments to implementing developmental teaching and learning within a classroom. They can occasionally even be implemented throughout an education department or school. However, developmental teaching and learning cannot be implemented in all the schools throughout a system without organizational integrity for the education program. This integrity is outside the grasp of the decentralized and bureau models, and can be attained best by a correctional school district. In both the earlier models, non-educators retained discretionary authority over the education program. This little-recognized relationship between the administrative system and the instructional system is an important dimension of the increased professionalization that is expected in correctional education during the culture period. How can instruction be innovative in an institutionalized administrative system? The school district model suggests a solution to this problem.

Internationalism

Another dimension of the culture period is its international focus. There has been a flurry of international attention directed to correctional education during recent years. European Prison Education Association conferences, not like the CEA international conferences (with only a few members from countries other than the United States), but conferences with truly international participation, have been held since 1989 at places like Oxford, Bergen (in the Netherlands), Brisbane, Estonia, Sophia, and in Denmark and Sweden. One is being planned for Dublin as this is written.

The International Forum for the Study of Education in Penal Systems (IFEPS) was established in 1991. IFEPS was a research consortium established by Stephen Duguid, with links to UNESCO and institutional members in Canada, the United States, Australia, and the United Kingdom. Since 1988 the United Nations has passed four resolutions to promote and improve prison reform and correctional education. Organizations like Prison Reform International and the International Adult Education Association publish informative newsletters and maintain a high level of international communication.

The national CEA established an executive board position for an international member, and an International Special Interest Group. The European Community established the European Prison Education Association, and new mass-membership organizations are being established elsewhere. More and more visitations, Fulbright Scholarships, teacher exchanges, and correspondences are being pursued by correctional educators from various nations—Turkey, New Zealand, Wales, Spain, the Czech Republic, England, Japan, Canada, Mexico, Nigeria, and so forth. Internationalism has become a major theme of correctional education.

Ultimately, internationalism can be the key that empowers correctional educators. Alienated in coercive institutions, often with non-educators in charge of the educational program, correctional educators have been extremely vulnerable. Historically, our uninformed status made us weak. Being informed about programs and strategies that have proven successful in other jurisdictions and nations, correctional educators are better equipped to maintain the integrity of the educational programs in the face of provincial views. Internationalism is an antidote for provincialism.

Third Generation Correctional Teacher Preparation Programs

The international theme is relevant to an emerging "third generation" of university-based correctional educator preparation programs, as well. Readers will recall that first generation programs were based on locally identified needs, and second generation programs were driven by the availability of Federal special education funds. Third generation programs will be based on the what works/best practices formula, from an international perspective.

The only third generation program in operation currently is at The Center for the Study of Correctional Education, at California State University, San Bernardino (an IFEPS member). The Center offers a masters degree in education with an emphasis on correctional and alternative education, and is based on the concept that the best correctional education practices from the United States and other nations can be forged together as a successful new North American correctional education paradigm.

Negative Impacts that Constrain Social Perception of These Positive Trends

The massive modifications in Title I No Child Left Behind Education Act in 2001 had a terribly negative impact on local public school education. The overall trend was that the differences experienced between correctional education and the local schools gradually washed away; teachers in the outside communities were quickly acquiring the perception that the milieu in which they worked had become fundamentally anti-education; local schools were being managed like little prisons. The effect on local school morale was a profound downward spiral, analogous to what correctional educators experience when the program goes through massive cutbacks and reductions in staffing.

However, correctional educators have had to be more resilient than public school educators in this episode. Correctional educators have traditionally been nearly alone in their classrooms, without adequate supervisory support, positive community interest in their work, even without access to what could be learned from the literature on correctional education—fighting merely to keep the program alive. Although most local school educators had never experienced a resource-rich environment, they had grown accustomed to moderate levels of support. By contrast, most correctional educators had learned through past practice that they would never receive the support they need or deserve, that they had to support each other if they would ever have a chance of living up to the responsibilities of their difficult but rewarding jobs.

Elements of this general assault on education included the following: (a) a blaming the victim approach toward teachers, in which it was assumed that teacher ineptitude and laziness was the root cause of poor basic skills acquisition (no new methods or resources were introduced, just an expectation that teachers needed to "do better"), (b) resultant de-skilling approach, in which scripted lessons and frequent monitoring through high-stakes testing often replaced traditional community respect for teachers, (c) continuation of the patterns that had already been experienced in correctional education, such as a reduction of all learning opportunities to a simple, measurable focus on basic and marketable skills (accompanied with huge cutbacks in subjects such as music, science, vocational education, and other curriculum components that became known as frills), (d) continuation of the vast underfunded mandates inherent in the special education laws, (e) a general neglect of the educational needs of traditionally disadvantaged groups, and of the aspiration for equal access to educational opportunity, (f) continued emphasis on superficial refinements of teacher licensure standards, based on the assumption that teachers do not deserve the benefit of the doubt, and should not be allowed to practice professional judgment in the classroom, (g) classroom overcrowding of such intensity that even seasoned educators felt hardpressed to meet even minimal job expectations, no less the new burdens that were heaped upon them, and (h) repeated assaults on teaching, designed at least in part to usher in a new age of vouchers and school privatization. In short, teachers in the local schools were being treated much as correctional educators had been treated for decades. Teaching was much less fun and rewarding than it had been just a few years before. Teachers were leaving the profession in great numbers, and university teacher credential programs reported record low enrollments.

The implementation of No Child Left Behind in corrections has been intermittent. A few states jumped in early and began reworking the correctional education infrastructure in line with the new law. Most states, however, did not. This staggered and incomplete implementation pattern resembled the long incubation period between passage of PL-94-142 and its associated legislation and its implementation "inside." Nevertheless, nearly everyone in corrections saw NCLB coming, and wondered if or when its mandates would be applied. For example, there was continued focus on just what the Highly Qualified Teacher mandate would look like in correctional education; this question has not been adequately answered to date. Several aspects of the law, such as school choice, are not possible to implement at all.

All these trends were exacerbated by the rising cost-of-war phenomenon (COW), which depleted funds from investments in all the infrastructures that foster human development. The anticipated "peace dividend" after the end of the Cold War, in which resources which had been directed to the arms race would hopefully be redirected to positive programming when the United States became the world's only superpower, never materialized. Rather, the U.S. invaded Panama, then Iraq, then the Balkans, and so forth, and then Afghanistan and Iraq again, and the forecast called for a more or less institutionalization of this stepped-up rate of deficit war expenditure for decades to come. It was explained as the cost of a new and protracted war on terror.

The fact that war was a Federal activity did not save states and local jurisdictions from direct experience of the cutback milieu, since Federal pass-through funds to other jurisdictions were slashed repeatedly to accommodate increased costs of military initiatives, as well as an overcrowded and burgeoning corrections industry, despite reductions in crime rates. For example, many states redirected funds from higher education in the exact proportion they directed it to corrections—sometimes with reductions in the numbers of professors exactly proportional to the increase in corrections officers. Funds were taken from safety net programs, and from those that helped humans grow and develop and feel personally secure, and spent on influences that had a morbid effect on communities: war and incarceration.

The impact of all this has been easily observed, though many professed not to see it because they were caught up in the passions of the moment, fear of criminals, terrorists, and often immigrants—anyone who could be defined as "the other." Nevertheless, the gradual creep of these trends accelerated into a significant reduction in services around 2003, when the war in the Mideast was prioritized. It may be that 2003 was the beginning of a new period in correctional education, defined by the COW and its correlates. However, this story is still unfolding, and the 2006 midterm elections may have signaled a shift in course. The No Child Left Behind Act comes up for consideration again in 2007; already at least 17 states have decided to reject Federal pass-through funding from this Act because of its negative effects on teaching and learning. For now, at least in relation to the history of correctional education and prison reform, the most we can do is to monitor these trends, and hope that the apparent magnitude of the slippage will be corrected, that the forces that propel humans toward their aspirations will become stronger than the forces that constrain them.

Summary and Conclusion

The culture period agenda is difficult to define because it is formative and ongoing. However, its main attributes, at least to the extent that they can be identified at this writing, are consistent with the professional aspirations expressed by many correctional educators. This marks a change from the aspirations that were expressed in the past, mostly by administrators—many of whom were not advocates of education. Though subtle, this has been a massive shift that should encourage correctional educators to continue their excellent endeavors to improve the world through strategies that improve educational services for confined learners. However, constraints on human potential have gathered strength and form, seemingly in proportion with those that would foster opportunities. Like the human condition itself, the state of prison reform and correctional education continues to be a grand adventure, a life and death gamble on the future of mankind.

References

Braithwaite, J. (1980). *Prisons, education, and work: Towards a national employment strategy for prisoners*. Queensland, Australia: University of Queensland Press.

Brockway, Z. (1969/1912). *Fifty years of prison service: An autobiography*. Montclair, New Jersey: Patterson Smith.

Dickens, C. (1957/1842). *American notes*. London: Oxford University Press, 97-111.

Freedman, E. (1981). *Their sister's keepers: Women's prison reform in America, 1830-1930*. Ann Arbor: University of Michigan Press.

Freire, P. (2001). *Pedagogy of the oppressed*. New York: Continuum International Publishing Group.

Freire, P. (2005). *Education for critical consciousness*. New York: Continuum.

George, W. (1911). *The Junior Republic: Its history and ideals*. New York: D. Appleton.

Guelzo, A.C. (2005). *The American mind*. Chantilly, Virginia: The Teaching Company (aucio CDs).

Jenkins, W.O. et al. (1972). *A manual for the use of the environmental deprivation scale (EDS) in corrections: The prediction of criminal behavior*. Springfield, Virginia: National Technical Information Service.

Kendall, G. (1939). *The organization and teaching of social and economic studies in correctional institutions*. New York: Bureau of Publications, Teachers College, Columbia University.

Knowles, M.S. (1970). *The modern practice of adult education: Andragogy versus pedagogy*. New York: Association Press.

Lowry, D. (1912). *My life in prison*. New York: John Lane.

Lozoff, B. (director) (1976). *Inside out: A spiritual manual for prison life*. Nederland, Colorado: Prison-Ashram Project. Note: Prison-Ashram is now located in Durham, North Carolina.

Lozoff, B. (1985). *We're all doing time*. Durham, NC: Human Kindness Foundation.

MacCormick, A. (1931). *The education of adult prisoners*. New York: The National Society of Penal Information.

Makarenko, A.S. (1954). *A book for parents*. Moscow: Foreign Languages Publishing House.

Makarenko, A.S. (1973). *The road to life: An epic in education*. New York: Oriole. (Three volumes).

McKelvey, B. (1977). *American prisons: A history of good intentions*. Montclair, New Jersey: Patterson Smith.

McMillan, J. and Schumachor, S. (2001). *Research in education: A conceptual introduction*. New York: Longman

Monroe, P.M. (1912). *A brief course on the history of education*. New York: MacMillan.

Murton, T.O. (1969). *Accomplices to the Crime: The Arkansas Prison Scandal*. New York: Grove Press.

Murton, T.O. (1976). *The dilemma of prison reform*. New York: Holt, Rinehart and Winston.

Nelson, C.M., Rutherford, R.B., and Wolford, B.I. (1987). *Special education in the criminal justice system*. Columbus, Ohio: Merrill.

O'Hare, K.R. (1923). *In prison*. New York: Knopf.

Osborne, T.M. (1924b). *Prisons and common sense*. Philadelphia: J.B. Lippincott.

Osborne, T.M. (1975/1916). *Society and prisons: Some suggestions for a new penology*. Montclair, New Jersey: Patterson Smith.

Osborne, T.M. (1924a). *Within prison walls*. New York: D. Appleton.

Rafter, N.H. (1985). *Partial Justice: Women in State Prisons, 1800-1935*. Boston: Northeastern University Press.

Ross, R., and Fabiano, E. (1985). *Time to think: A cognitive model of delinquency prevention and offender rehabilitation*. Johnson City, Tennessee: Institute of Social Sciences and Arts.

Scudder, K.J. (1968/1952). *Prisoners are people*. New York: Greenwood Press.

Seashore, M., and Haberfeld, S. (1976). *Prisoner education: Project NewGate and other college programs*. New York: Praeger.

Tannenbaum, F. (1933). *Osborne of Sing Sing*. Chapel Hill: University of North Carolina Press.

Twain, M. (2001/1894). *The trajedy of Puddin'head Wilson.* Sandy, Utah: Quiet Vision Publishing.

Wallack, W. (ed.). (1939). *Correctional education today.* New York: American Prison Association.

Wallack, W. (ed.). (1940). *Prison administration—An educational process.* New York: American Prison Association.

Wallack, W. (ed.). (1937). *The training of prison guards.* New York: Teachers College, Columbia University (unpublished dissertation).

Wines, E.C. (ed.). (1871). *Transactions of the National Congress on Penitentiary and Reformatory Discipline.* Albany: Argus.

Wallack, W., Kendall, G., and Briggs, H. (1939). *Education within prison walls.* New York: Bureau of Publications, Teachers College, Columbia University.

Werner, D. (1990). *Correctional Education: Theory and practice.* Danville, Illinois: Interstate Publishers.

Acknowledgements

Excerpts from *Prisons, Education, and Work: Towards a National Employment Strategy for Prisoners* by J. Braithwaite, copyright © 1980 University of Queensland Press. Excerpts from *Fifty Years of Prison Service: An Autobiography* by Z. Brockway, copyright © 1969/1912 Patterson Smith. Excerpts from *American Notes* by C. Dickens, copyright © 1957/1842 Oxford University Press. Excerpts from *Their Sister's Keepers: Women's Prison Reform in America, 1830-1930* by E. Freedman, copyright © 1981 University of Michigan Press. Excerpts from *Pedagogy of the Oppressed* by P. Freire, copyright © 2001 Continuum. Excerpts from *Education for Critical Consciousness* by P. Freire, copyright © 2005 Continuum. Excerpts from *The Junior Republic: Its History and Ideals* by W. George, copyright © 1911 D. Appleton. Excerpts from *A Manual for the use of the Environmental Deprivation Scale (EDS) in Corrections: The Prediction of Criminal Behavior* by W.O. Jenkins, et al. copyright © 1972 National Technical Information Service. Excerpts from *The Organization and Teaching of Social and Economic Studies in Correctional Institutions* by G. Kendall, copyright © 1939 Teachers College, Columbia University. Excerpts from *The Modern Practice of Adult Education: Andragogy versus Pedagogy* by M.S. Knowles, copyright © 1970 Association Press. Excerpts from *My Life in Prison* by D. Lowry, copyright © 1912 John Lane. Excerpts from *Inside Out: A Spiritual Manual for Prison Life* by B. Lozoff (director), copyright © 1976 Prison-Ashram Project. Excerpts from *We're All Doing Time* by B. Lozoff, copyright © 1985 Human Kindness Foundation. Excerpts from *The Education of Adult Prisoners* by A. MacCormick, copyright © 1931 The National Society of Penal Information. Excerpts from *A Book for Parents* by A.S. Makarenko, copyright © 1954 Foreign Languages Publishing House. Excerpts from *The Road to Life: an Epic in Education* by A.S. Makarenko, copyright © 1973 Oriole. Excerpts from *American Prisons: a History of Good Intentions* by B. McKelvey, copyright © 1977 Patterson Smith. Excerpts from *A Brief Course on the History of Education* by P.M. Monroe, copyright © 1912 MacMillan. Excerpts from *Accomplices to the Crime: the Arkansas Prison Scandal* by T.O. Murton, copyright © 1969 Grove Press. Excerpts from *The Dilemma of Prison Reform* by T.O. Murton, copyright © 1976 Holt, Rinehart and Winston. Excerpts from *Special Education in the Criminal Justice System* by C.M. Nelson, R.B. Rutherford, and B.I. Wolford, copyright © 1987 Merrill. Excerpts from *In Prison* by K.R. O'Hare, copyright © 1923 Knopf. Excerpts from *Prisons and Common Sense* by T.M. Osborne, copyright © 1924 J.B. Lippincott Company. Reprinted by permission of HarperCollins Publishers. Excerpts from *Society and Prisons: Some Suggestions for a New Penology* by T.M. Osborne, copyright © 1975/1916 Patterson Smith. Excerpts from *Within Prison Walls* by T.M. Osborne, copyright © 1924 D. Appleton. Excerpts from *Partial Justice: Women in State Prisons, 1800-1935* by N.H. Rafter, copyright © 1985 Northeastern University Press. Excerpts from *Time to Think: a Cognitive Model of Delinquency Prevention and Offender Rehabilitation* by R. Ross and E. Fabiano, copyright © 1985 Institute of Social Sciences and Arts. From *Prisoners are People* by K.J. Scudder, copyright © 1952 by Franklin F. Scudder. Used by permission of Doubleday, a division of Random House, Inc. Excerpts from *Prisoner Education: Project NewGate and other College Programs* by M. Seashore and S. Haberfeld, copyright © 1976 Praeger. Excerpts from *Osborne of Sing Sing* by F. Tannenbaum copyright © 1933

University of North Carolina Press. Excerpts from *The Tragedy of Puddin'head Wilson* by M. Twain, copyright © 2001/1894 Quiet Vision Publishing. Excerpts from *Correctional Education Today* by W. Wallack (ed.), copyright © 1939 American Prison Association. Excerpts from *Prison Administration—An Educational Process* by W. Wallack (ed.), copyright © 1940 American Prison Association. Excerpts from *The Training of Prison Guards* by W. Wallack (ed.), copyright © 1937 Teachers College, Columbia University. Excerpts from *Transactions of the National Congress on Penitentiary and Reformatory Discipline* by E.C. Wines, (ed.), copyright © 1871 Argus. Excerpts from *Education Within Prison Walls* by W. Wallack, G. Kendall, and H. Briggs, copyright © 1939 Bureau of Publications, Teachers College, Columbia University. Excerpts from *Correctional Education: Theory and Practice* by D. Werner, copyright © 1990 Interstate Publishers.